Timeri N. Murari began his career as a reporter on a Candian newspaper before moving to London to write for *The Guardian, The Sunday Times* and other newspapers, and magazines. He has since written novels, non-fiction books, a young adult trilogy, stage plays and screenplays. *Time* included his film, *Daayra,* in its top 10 films of the year. His novel *TAJ, A Story of Mughal India* has been translated into twenty-five languages, and *The Taliban Cricket Club* into eight.

AF652072

Works by Timeri N. Murari

Novels

The Marriage

The Oblivion Tapes

Lovers Are Not People

Field of Honour (re-titled)
Gunboat Jack, A Novel

The Shooter

TAJ, A Story of Mughal India

The Imperial Agent

The Last Victory

Enduring Affairs

Four Steps from Paradise

The Arrangements of Love

The Small House

The Taliban Cricket Club

Chankaya Returns

A Country of No Return

Non-fiction

The New Savages

Goin' Home, A Black Family Returns South

My Temporary Son

Limping to the Centre of the World

Young Adult

Children of the Enchanted Jungle

Axxiss and the Magic Medallions

Axxiss and the Undersea Kingdon

Axxiss and the Parallel Universe

Harvey and Melville, Detectives

Films & Television

The Square Circle (Daayra)

The Only Thing

Television trilogy: Only an America

Plays

The Inquisitor

Hey Hero!

The Square Circle (also directed)

The Assasination of an Unknown Writer

Killing Time

Enter Queen Lear

Editor

The Evil Within

Empress of the TAJ

In Search of Mumtaz Mahal

TIMERI N. MURARI

SPEAKING TIGER

SPEAKING TIGER PUBLISHING PVT. LTD
4381/4, Ansari Road, Daryaganj
New Delhi 110002

First published by Speaking Tiger in paperback 2019

Copyright © Timeri N. Murari 2019

ISBN: 978-93-88874-64-9
eISBN: 978-93-88874-65-6

10 9 8 7 6 5 4 3 2 1

Typeset in Arno Pro by SÜRYA, New Delhi
Printed at Sanat Printers, Kundli

All rights reserved.

No part of this publication may be reproduced, transmitted, or stored in a retrieval system, in any form or by any means, electronic, mechanical, photocopying, recording or otherwise, without the prior permission of the publisher.

This book is sold subject to the condition that it shall not, by way of trade or otherwise, be lent, resold, hired out, or otherwise circulated, without the publisher's prior consent, in any form of binding or cover other than that in which it is published.

For my friend of many years, Rajeev, and for my constant travel companion, Maureen, with love.

What you've done becomes the judge of what you're going to do—especially in other people's minds. When you're traveling, you are what you are right there and then. People don't have your past to hold against you. No yesterdays on the road.

—William Least Heat-Moon

Contents

The Revelation

I discovered a book I had thought lost. It happens to writers. I was searching for a memory of my past in a trunk under the stairs and found a yellowing typed manuscript. Typed! That dated it and explained the amnesia. I had learned to write on a typewriter and thus belonged to an ancient era. I still have that Smith Corona, pale blue with sturdy keys that withstood the hammering to translate thoughts and longing into words on the paper in the roller. As a journalist, I had carried the machine around the world, a heavy weight in the overhead bins of planes. The edges of the manuscript curled with long neglect. An insect scuttled off the first page, no doubt snacking on my words. I wondered what story the pages told that I had forgotten and buried in the debris of my life. Was it a novel I had set aside, and never returned to finish the story? There is no title page. It is dated August 1986.

It begins:

'Waiting for the full moon to rise into a clear starry sky, and listening to the music of water in the fountains, I imagine her beauty. Her eyes would have been grey, not the clear, delicate shading of dawn light, but darker like the clouds massing for the monsoons. Her hair would have been an iridescent black, waist

length too and perfumed with sandalwood or attar of roses. Her skin would have been the colour of ivory, and her mouth sensual and passionate as… as…'

A love story? Who was the woman that enchanted me to begin a story with her description? I think back to past lovers and affairs. My memory is clear here; they are not forgotten. I hope they remember too, both the joy and the pain of the relationships. Eyes grey, two women appear in memory, distinctive despite the many years. I wonder where they are. Is this woman one of them? But they did not have 'iridescent' black hair, waist length. Shoulder length, but their hair was of a lighter colour, auburn, blonde. Not sandalwood or attar, not there in the cold climates of my past. Smelling more of Dior, Je Reviens, Joy on their skin. And all women are 'sensual and passionate as… as…' I appear to have run out of metaphors. Writers disguise their past lovers, changing skin, bones, cheeks, imagine her in a new avatar but keep to the very essence of those women the writer knew so long ago. Graham Greene wrote that 'Every writer has a splinter of ice in his heart'. Is this splinter the woman who begins the story? So far, this faded page stirs no memory as to why I wrote this manuscript that I excavated. Should I read on, spending time on the forgotten past, when I have work to do? I'll return it to lie where it was hidden so long ago. I'll read one more line…

'I cannot unravel the shroud of marble that has hidden her from the sight of man for so many centuries too swiftly. She was born and lived most of her life under this unassuming appellation but on her death she was immortalized forever under a different name. Her bones are encased in a sarcophagus

of yellowing marble, inlaid with delicately coloured flowers and green stems; all once studded with precious stones. Above her remains, glowing with ghostly solitude in pale moonlight, rises the high exquisite tomb...'

Eureka! Now I remember the book I wrote long ago and thought lost. She was the reason I wrote a novel, a work entirely of fiction, spun out of historical research and my imagination. This manuscript was the groundwork on which I created that fiction. This is the bricks, the mortar, the travels of that creative work, *TAJ, A Story of Mughal India,* which was published in 1985 in the UK and since then translated into twenty-five languages. I read on.

'I became obsessed by this mysterious woman, Arjumand, who so captivated the Mughal prince Shah Jahan that he loved her and only her and on her death stamped the earth in such sorrow that he left her imprint in marble. He called it Mumtaz Mahal.

'Who was she? I will tell you the story of this woman Arjumand and how she loved and how she eventually died, but first you must travel with me over 2000 miles through the cities and villages and jungles of India by train and by bus. It will be a journey that will take you many weeks and three hundred and fifty years before you stand by her original tomb on the banks of the river Tapti in Burhanpur. Burhanpur! I could not imagine this place myself. Where was this grave, this strange name implanted in the limbo of history perversely to distract my mind? The name itself conjures up heat, a few small buildings, a metallic lane linking one horizon to another, all lost in the shimmering haze of India.'

Nomad

But I must begin at the beginning and how the obsession took root. With a woman a glance, a glimpse, a voice, a whisper, a tendril of perfume is enough to grip the heart but Arjumand was beyond these senses. She was summoned from the grave out of pure pique. Her tomb was featured on the cover of a previous novel of mine, *Field of Honour*, for no reason other than it was set in India. I told my American editor, Michael Korda, that Agra was over 1000 miles from the Bangalore setting of the work. He shrugged, 'No one knows where India is. This identifies it.' So narrow is the Western publisher's perception of India. At least I had a quote from a writer I admired, and whose works I had read, to counter the cover. Graham Greene wrote, ' I was very much impressed with *Field of Honour*'. The tomb on my book cover stared at me for months and took root.

I lived in New York then, my home for thirteen years. Before that, in London. I was a stranger to India, a tourist, passing through. I had books, novels and non-fiction, published in the UK, US and some translated into European languages. On a visit, I had brought my bride, Maureen, to see the Taj Mahal. A deserted tourist sight then, so few visitors, we were alone at times, wandering the garden and the tomb. She asked for the story of the tomb. I gave her my schoolbook potted history of the Mughal empire. It wasn't enough. I was ignorant of my history, she teased. We returned to New York. Our apartment was a 15-minute bus ride away from the New York Public Library, that repository of every book published. In the catalogue also, every book known on the Mughals, and the Taj Mahal. I read everything, the antidote to my ignorance, just to tell Maureen the complete, detailed history. I had no intention of writing a book, non-fiction or fiction. I was wanting to start another book on India but my experience of spending four months following two homicide detectives, Andy Lugo and Tony Colon, in the 48th precinct in the South Bronx, blocked my mind. The streets there were darker than any Raymond Chandler had walked or imagined. This was for a documentary I was to write and apart from seeing the many ways people killed, I had also socialized days and nights in the bars with the cops. I knew their life stories. To cleanse my mind, I wrote a noir novel, *The Shooter*.

Like any writer, I hate wasting material. I was replete with Mughal history and the idea for a work of fiction wriggled slowly out of my consciousness. I had never written a historical novel before; my books, fiction and non-fiction, were set in contemporary times. I read a couple of historical novels, set in India, written by English authors. I tossed them aside, slanted in their view of India, slanted in their racial superiority. I picked up *I, Claudius* by Robert Graves, and read it cover to cover. It was a brilliant novel and that inspired me. I needed narrators for what I saw as a complex work, not just a love story but also a tragedy of power, betrayals and murders.

The beginning of the journey, in October 1982, was down south in Madras, a place Arjumand had never envisaged, so distant is it from Agra, although she did wander endlessly over the face of northern India. I understand the nomad well. As Arjumand wandered that Mughal empire, so my family in my early years zigged and zagged across the British one. The empires lay one upon the other, three-and-a-half centuries apart and yet physically and emotionally beside each other. The ruins of the old were scattered over the land, while the new had yet to leave a heritage of comparable magnificence. What better proof of our nomadic existence than my mother's death in Lahore, 2000 kilometres from our ancestral home in Madras. On a globe the distance in latitudes is 13 degrees to 32, El Salvador to Dallas, Texas. There is no grave or monument to her memory in Lahore, a place now beyond the frontiers of that old India. Her ashes were immersed in the snow-fed rivers and as they swirled and fragmented, I lost all memory of her. If my memories of her ceased to exist, my memory of those journeys remain but as fragments, torn bits of a map, the edges darkened by funeral flames; ashes, afloat in the breeze. Lahore, Meerut, Simla, Delhi, Agra, Dehra Doon, Ajmer, Jhansi, Hyderabad, Bangalore, Madras. The odour of petrol and places, cars, trains, lorries and jutkas, a ceaseless blur of India and as I grew older they grew more distinct, emerging, it seemed, from the gloom of death. Where in India as a child had I not been? Burhanpur.

My authorities on the twists and turns, the mysterious

and enchanting, the fake and the genuine of India have been either my father or my sister Nalini. At some point in time, my father has been there or here, having spent years wandering India, first as an army officer, later as a government official, and then in yet another guise as a supplicant in search of God's physical presence on earth. He has wandered the world too but now in old age he has quite forgotten the existence of other countries. They have just ceased to be. Though now and then in his nomadic thoughts, he will pop up in Oxford or Aberystwyth, New York or Sydney, Rome or Greece, quite puzzled by his surroundings before hurrying to return to India. Nalini, my sister, as boundlessly energetic as our father, is also an authority on the land. Her love for India is transparent. She is steeped not only in its history, but in the mythology of our religion too and if I should not remember which avatar is which she is quick to lecture me on the intricacies of religious genealogy. But this place called Burhanpur also puzzles her and her curiosity aroused, she decides to join me later on this quest for a grave.

Sitting in the shade of an ancient neem tree in our garden, my father vaguely recalls Burhanpur. It rings a chord for him but those chords now are illusionary strings. He says he might have been there but it sounds like a hundred other places in India—Kanpur, Sholapur, Jaipur, Raipur and possibly in the confusion of years, he believes he had also been to Burhanpur. He tries to describe it to me and fails. It's possible this place is so featureless that there is no stirring landmark to describe; nothing there apart from this forgotten grave to cling to the chords of memory.

We possess a world atlas, one of those huge, multi-coloured volumes given away by publishers in search of magazine sales. I'm sure Burhanpur exists in those gloriously coloured pages but I cannot bring myself to consult it. I choose instead an old and familiar map of India. It lies enclosed in a dusty plastic case. It has a hard cover, the size of a decent-length novel and the gold lettering, *A Road Map of India,* has faded to a blur. When you open the book, a colourful 4-foot square map unfolds, revealing towns, roads, railway lines and rivers, named in small print that needs a magnifying glass to read at times. It has a white hessian cloth backing and was printed by the Survey of India in 1943. It is filled with nostalgia. How many times I remember as a child, stranded on a strange road, we would unfold this map on the bonnet of our car and try to discover our precise location. Swiftly, as these things happen in India, we would be surrounded by curious villagers who were of little help. They knew their village and the next, but beyond that India disappeared over the horizon. The map has survived countless journeys, unfolded and folded, mishandled by children too impatient to have the care to fold it back in the way it was meant to fold. Other books, even a whole set of *Encyclopaedia Britannica,* have been mislaid in our nomadic life but my father has somehow clung to this. Even now he watches with a frown of worry as I spread it open on the dining table. I unfold a British vision of my India. It is an act of peering back in time, a shift in perception and history in which the names of thousands of roads, rivers, towns, villages, valleys and mountains were distorted in order to facilitate an alien tongue. Ganges, Jumna, Cawnpore,

Poona, Conjeevaram, Benares have now reverted back to their original incarnations—Ganga, Yamuna, Kanpur, Pune, Kanchipuram, Varanasi—as India sloughs off this chaotic mutation of her past. Of course, in this old map the north west, where my mother died, is all still a part of India. The pattern of the landscape remains familiar while artificial borders have now been slashed into this ancient body. Familiar! To believe this is illusion. Nothing in India can be familiar, the silt of history lies too deep on the land. Burhanpur, now forgotten, is hidden within the fold marks of the map.

Burhanpur was, from 1556 to 1707, the southern capital of the Mughal empire. Akbar, Humayun, Jahangir, Shah Jahan, Aurangzeb, emperors with unimaginable wealth and power, spent years of their lives in this elusive town. How they discovered it in this vastness is quite incomprehensible. It was once a kind of Luxor, stranded on another shoal of history, but finding it, like a word you cannot spell, is not an easy matter.

There is a clue. In 1614 Sir Thomas Roe, the first English ambassador from the court of James I, sailed up the Tapti to present his credentials to Emperor Jahangir's second son, Parwez, who was then Subadar of the Deccan. Roe was, by all accounts, an adventurous but arrogant man. He strutted around with European superiority, refusing to bow according to court protocol, and keeping up a barrage of complaints about his accommodation. If only Jahangir had managed to peep into the future, he would not have been so kind and patient with this stranger. Roe sailed from the town of Surat, which lies north of Bombay below the Indian armpit. Surat is another place stranded in history, dreaming in the heat of those heady days when the Portuguese fought fiercely to keep their toehold on Indian soil. They were a nuisance to the Mughals but, as a major sea power, a necessity. They offered the most convenient route to Mecca. By sea it took one third the time and was far less hazardous than the overland route. It was the medieval equivalent of flying. But the Portuguese insisted on issuing the Muslim pilgrims a 'passport' stamped with a picture of the Virgin Mary. This offended the Mughal Muslims for it was considered sacrilege to carry the image of another religion on their persons. But there was little they could do about it.

The Tapti on my map is a thin wriggling blue line that rises in the Vindhya mountains of central India and empties itself into the Arabian sea. I trace back along its course, passing tiny roads and bridges, past Kathor, Mandivi, Taloda, Shahada, Shirpur, Yaval, Bhusawai ... Burhanpur!

It lies near the belly button of India and looks quite inaccessible on this map, except by road. There is a railway line curling past it but it is difficult to tell how near. In India these things are never quite precise. It is a centimetre on the map but it could be miles. The major cities nearby are Indore to the north and Nagpur to the west. Nagpur, roughly measured by a finger's width, looks the closest except the road abruptly ends on one side of the Tapti. Burhanpur is on the other side.

Possibly in the intervening 40 years since the map was printed, a bridge has been built across the Tapti but in India 40 years doesn't necessarily mean a bridge has been thrown across to convenience my journey. I imagine the end of the metalled road, like a severed nerve, still lapped by the water, forgotten by those who built it so many years ago. And modern India too preoccupied to return to it. It would have to be from Indore that I journeyed to Arjumand's grave but Burhanpur, as it was for her, would be at the very end of the road.

The Start

The beginning for my journey was down south in Madras. Train journeys in India are never undertaken lightly, especially the complex route I planned to follow. An Indian train is my cure for insomnia. I have spent countless nights comforted by the rhythmical rocking, lulled by the constant whir of fans and breathing the familiar odours of Indian dust. Six times a year, twice for each term, I came and went from Madras Central station to Bangalore Cantonment. I would be placed on the Madras Mail, leaving at 9 p.m. Then, burdened with a battered black trunk which had my name stencilled in white on all sides and a holdall. This was the bulky forerunner of the sleeping bag. It was a canvas contraption that contained a cotton mattress and it had large pockets at either end for pillows, pyjamas, shoes, books and any odds and ends that failed to fit into the trunk. It made a bumpy bed and at times I would wake in sudden stillness and peer through the iron bars of the window to look out on a dark and deserted landscape, frosted with moonlight. The very silence and emptiness of India asleep filled me with awe. The sky curved interminably overhead, bent on its own voyage. Far ahead, the engine steamed and hissed in patient waiting. Other sleepers around me stirred but slept on and like the engine I would wait. For what it waited, I never discovered. There were no signals, no swaying lanterns. Only the vast, mysterious night. Then, just as suddenly, it would huff-huff and start off again. The fans never ceased their whirr and the memory of them still lulls me to sleep. It was a womb of metal and wood.

India naturally is proud to boast of the third largest railway system in the world. However, our railways were designed by the English for a tiny England, they were meant to run between Cheltenham and Bath, not a thousand miles across a harsh land. If the Russians or the Canadians, the one and two of railways, had built this system, they would have, drawing on the vastness of their own land, constructed huge carriages and wide tracks to carry our millions. But it's too late for such thoughts and the trains have changed since my schooldays. Diesel and electricity have taken the place of steam and the compartments have shrunk. Nalini, my sister, is more nostalgic than me on this subject: 'What trains we had in those days! You, of course, wouldn't remember. They were all wood-panelled, teak or mahogany and all the handles and taps were brass. The seats were also real leather. As a family we'd take a whole compartment to ourselves and we had our own private bathroom attached and it was big enough to also have a shower stall.' I keep trying to keep her off stage, to await her turn in the natural order of this book when she joins us later in Delhi but she can be a most impatient woman.

Madras Central has a red façade, both Mughal and Victorian. There are turrets on either end but beyond this grand exterior, the cavernous hangar is quite chaotic with the hustle and bustle of travellers and trains. Like the pregnant city, it has swollen over the years, voraciously consuming space where possible. The only way it could expand was across the stagnant and smelly Coome river into Moore Market. In some ways they are deceptively alike in architecture. Sort of Indo-Saracenic with turrets and pillars. Moore Market has a red-brick face and archways, and was a large rectangle, built around a garden courtyard. Sir George Moore, president of Madras Corporation, laid the foundation stone in 1898. I spent much of my childhood wandering through the stalls of this bazaar buying schoolbooks, toys, comics and years later, especially at the rear, a jumble of antiques that a modern India no longer had much use for: a 19th-century camera, a marble Maha Vishnu, a valuable Tanjore painting, an ivory Krishna.

The voyage into the paperwork begins at the entrance to the station, shuttling between the countless windows clutching pen, forms and railway timetables. One for the north, another for the south, a further division between us and them. The timetables are packed with detailed instructions: how to book journeys, how to get bedding, which stations have waiting rooms, the various kinds of tickets, reservations. And of course the times, destinations, halts of the thousands of trains that criss-cross the subcontinent. As I'm not making a single-destination journey I need to study the timetable with the same care and concern a punter gives his betting sheet. One mistake and all the paperwork will have to be re-done, telegrams sent to distant station-masters informing them that Murari isn't coming on that day but the next and the escalating costs of cancellations and re-bookings. The names of the trains still resound with steam and more adventurous days. The one from Madras to Delhi is still called the Grand Trunk Express, and it has been making its daily 1000-mile run for decades. In my childhood, it took days to crawl up the face of India but now the journey is done in a flash. Well, a long flash. A mere 36 hours for it to rush north to our capital. But I have also travelled on many others in the past, equally exotic in name and destination: the Frontier Mail, the Doon Express, the Brindavan Express, the Jammu-Tawi, the Tamilnad Express, the Howrah Mail, the Deccan Queen and even as I inscribe these names I still feel the excitement of those journeys. For each train we are to take, another form is filled with name of train, number, up/down, name of passenger, sex, age, signature. I have never discovered why age and sex are so essential but miss one out and the clerk barricaded behind his counter, surrounded by huge leather-bound ledgers that resemble doomsday books, will toss the form back. His columns must be filled, over and over again. Due to some long-forgotten custom, doubtless introduced by the British to help memsahibs get preferential treatment among us natives, women can queue jump. As mostly males clog the window, it is easy for my wife, Maureen, to push ahead. The clerk, a middle-aged man with spectacles and a neat moustache, looks at all the forms, and begins inscribing my journey in those ledgers. It's like watching the moving finger write.

'Ahhh, you cannot travel from Nagpur to Burhanpur,' he suddenly announces, and waits patiently for my question, 'Why not?' 'Nagpur is on the Delhi line. Burhanpur on the

Calcutta line,' he answers triumphantly as if he has waited patiently just for me to ask that question. Maybe we have been pre-destined. He looks comforted. Triumphs are rare in a clerk's life and he savours it as he would a morsel of paan. 'They do not cross.'

Like my road, there is no bridge. The two are separate until eternity. I take back the forms, fill them in again. I will have to make the journey from Indore.

I slide my American Express card across the counter. He stares at it for a very long moment, before finally deciding that it is safe for him to pick it up. He reads the front, then the back, quite bemused and puzzled by this bit of plastic. I know American Express is not accepted everywhere and skim across my Visa card. He performs the same close examination, reading it as if I've given him a long, incomprehensible novel to decipher.

'What are these?' he asks, finally.

'Credit cards. They are acceptable everywhere.' I know I am quoting a commercial.

'Credit cards.' He savours the words, then passes them back to me, and says patiently, as if addressing an idiot, 'Cash.'

I retreat and return the next day with 'Cash' and my forms. He takes the cash, counts and re-counts it and only then does he start filling in his ledger and making out all those tickets.

I have also reached the age for comfort and there is no greater luxury than making the long haul to Delhi in air-conditioning. It's not merely the heat but the smothering dust which changes the complexion of blondes to brunettes and black hair to a peculiar red and where sweat cuts visible furrows through grime. Before air-conditioning, each compartment had a large trough in which a massive cake of ice would be placed. Nalini tells me, 'Padmini (my other sister) and I would sit on the block of ice to keep cool but all that ever happened was that we got frozen bottoms.' Class, as inherited from the British—'European Only', First, Second and Third—have been replaced by the complex and convoluted philosophy of modern India. We now have first and second, third doubtless abolished because of its connotations, but above first we now have a/c sleeper, a dormitory for forty-six and a/c upper, privilege coupes. The air-conditioned carriages, like incognito movie stars, have double-glazed, smoked windows. Our sleeper is divided into fours, two up two down with the narrow passage fitted with one down and one up. Forty-six bunks in all, though not crammed in, certainly do make one uncomfortably aware of one's fellow travellers.

Our berth numbers are posted at the entrance and we find ourselves sharing with an elderly couple. The wife glances at me, then Maureen, and visibly curls herself away into the corner. She is plump, with a strong face, not a fading beauty, and I suspect an orthodox Hindu filled with more neurotic tics than a dog has fleas. Her eyes had briefly whirred with the slot machine of prejudices—caste, colour, language, town, village. Doubtless Maureen is untouchable and me too for having her for a wife. I find myself slotted in—three lemons—and dismissed. Her husband, equally round and comfortable but with a gentler face, smiles cheerfully at us. 'We are going to Agra,' he says as we settle on the lower bunk. ('For the convenience of other passengers please do not use as bed between the hours of 8 a.m. and 9 p.m.') 'We were in Madras visiting relatives. I'm a retired government servant. I was in the forest division.' His life unfolds as easily as a map, one of service, security, retirement and death. He has fulfilled his dharmas and is satisfied that nothing much more is expected of him in life.

I sketch my life briefly: birth place, Madras; school, Bangalore; college, Madras and abroad; am also going to Agra and then to Burhanpur; and recognize the instant glaze that veils his eyes when I fill in the blank for profession: journalist/writer. We are fairly low in the totem of Indian social esteem and I know for sure I'd never be offered their daughter's hand in marriage. Government servant, IAS officer would have them grovelling at my feet. A doctor too or an engineer with an American passport would have them showering lakhs of rupees on my head as dowry.

The Journey

At precisely 6.15 p.m. the Grand Trunk Express slides out of Central Station. The tinted windows darken our fading twilight into a grey blur. The first few miles are familiar as I've passed by here countless times but Madras is no longer the slim and pretty girl, the Bharatanatyam dancer, of my youth. She has lost her beauty and her grace, grown fat, blowsy and higgledy-piggledy. She bulges with gross dewlaps of concrete flesh. Rice fields and villages and open maidans have become factory-ized and housing colony-ized. We have discovered concrete and tarmac with a vengeance. But night thankfully comes swiftly and all the ugliness of 'progress' vanishes into the reflection of our faces peering out.

Outside the cocoon of chilly, sterilized air, India swirls in the corridor. Moist heat, dust, a rush of noise and smells and the land comes back into existence through the open windows. We rush through darkness, suddenly coming upon a blare of lights and life, a distant truck cutting the darkness delicately with headlights and in the distance a flicker of electric bulbs. But beyond this immediate vision, beyond undulating hills that fade into the sky, are still the villages keeping this great and insatiable darkness at bay with the flicker of oil lamps, waiting for the electric wires to reach them. India's needs, like the sky, are forever limitless.

I'm joined by a slim, ascetic-looking man. He looks to be in his well-preserved sixties, wears a clean and well-pressed dhoti and jiba. He also has the scrubbed air of a Brahmin.

'What do you do?' he cuts to the chase. We like to pigeon-hole each other as quickly as possible.

'A journalist.' I leave out writer. In the old days, writers were clerks under British rule. Clive was a writer, though he didn't write a word and only looted India with his sword.

He looks pleased. 'I have worked all my life in *The Hindu*. I was secretary to the editor. I retired five years ago and am accompanying my daughter to Mathura. She is an extraordinary woman. She did her BA first class honours and has now completed her doctorate in Hindu philosophy. She recites the Vedas every morning and also composes a new prayer each morning in Sanskrit. How these prayers come are only known to the Divine. She is an expert on the Vedas and has travelled the world—we went to Singapore—to give lectures. Now she will lecture in Mathura, Delhi, Agra and Varanasi.'

I retreat under this onslaught of information. He has spoken with the fervour of a disciple and this woman appears to have been elevated to divinity. He devotes his retired life attending to her needs and I suspect he wants me to present myself and receive darshan. Instead, when we return to the compartment, I walk eyes ahead, with only the swiftest of glances in her direction. She is a plump young woman, sitting cross-legged and surrounded by her disciples, softly singing bhajans. My companion looks at me in deep disapproval. I have ignored the opportunity of a lifetime but he is not to know I have met so many 'holy' men and women that I can be somewhat blasé. Our home in Madras is almost an ashram as my father entertains all and sundry who land up on our doorstep. Child saints, saffroned sadhus on the con, American lady divines, miracle men, and countless others—astrologers and jugglers, wandering minstrels and magicians. I've developed, sadly, a cynical seismograph at their approach, for the 'miracles' they perform are sleights-of-hand and their divinity usually insists on generous donations. In these encounters I've always emerged poorer, financially and spiritually. My father, however, retains an unbounded enthusiasm for all these charlatans sustained by the belief that, finally, one of them will be the genuine article. He will find him or her long before I ever will, for he's blessed with an unwavering faith.

As a people, we Indians pursue our superstitions with unbounding zeal. And why not? Hinduism has 330 million deities in its pantheon of gods, one for every three people. An extravagant and confusing generosity. Of course these deities are all illusion. The British, after a century in India, polled us idolaters and published their findings in the *Imperial Gazetteer* of 1901: 'The general result of my enquiries,' wrote a Mr Burns, 'is that the great majority of Hindus have a firm belief in One Supreme God, called Bhagvan, Parameshwar, Ishwar, or Narain. Mr Baillie made some enquiries which showed that this involved a clear idea of a single personal God, and I am inclined to think that this is distinctly characteristic of Hindus as a whole.'

At eight, as the Grand Trunk slides along the eastern coastline towards Guntur, the bearers move quickly and efficiently through the train serving dinner. The food—chicken curry, vegetable, dhall, rice, chapatis—manifests itself in compartmentalized aluminium trays. The rocking train however has mixed it all up. The cooking is good but the portions surprisingly too much. The bearers are followed by the train attendant, distributing bedding—sheets, blankets, pillow and a towel—to those in need. As most have the old familiar hold-all, we are the only takers. The sheets are vaguely white, wafting the powerful odour of soap powder. As I settle down for the night on the upper bunk, with Maureen opposite, for the old couple, claiming the right of age, cannot make the climb, I wish I had my old hold-all and cotton mattress. The berth has only vague pretentions to softness beneath the vinyl.

At dawn, I sip my coffee in the outside corridor, watching the sun rising and the great landscape unfolding. India was imagined and shaped on a massive, craggy scale. We have passed Vijayawada in the night and the delicious green rice fields slipping past, with men and women absorbed in their infinitely ancient ways of labour, while children tend scraggy cattle and wave to the train as it rushes on, soon begin to give way to hills. Jungles of impenetrable thorn and twisted trees crowd in on the track. Miles pass, the sunlight filtering through this thinning foliage, without a human in sight—a rare occurrence. It is another illusion for when you believe yourself totally alone in the vastness of India, a girl, a boy, a knot of people will slowly materialize out of nowhere to stare curiously, silently at you. I am not, in some other scale of Darwinian evolution, that distanced from the village. Apart from childhood on a farm, my ancestral village, Timeri—from which my great grandfathers emerged into urban life—is a two-hour journey from Madras. It is a pretty little place, surrounded by rice fields and coconut palms, in which a few relatives lead calm and placid lives.

We are now in the Satmala hills nearing Nagpur and the centre of India. These hills were part of the Vindhya range and were the barrier to the Mughal empire's extension south towards Hyderabad, once called Golconda. For two centuries the Mughal emperors—Akbar, Jahangir, Shah Jahan—made attempts to conqueror the Golconda kings. It was not merely the greed for territory but for the great riches of this kingdom. When their descendant Aurangzeb finally did make the breakthrough in the mid-17th century, the plunder from Golconda was said to equal the wealth of the Mughal treasury. And somewhere west of here, beyond the hazy, shimmering hills is the town of Burhanpur, the launching pad for these military expeditions. The Grand Trunk does not stop often on its long haul north but when it does I can never resist getting out to wander the platforms. Here India mingles: Sikh, Jat, hill tribe, Tamil, Punjabi, Pathan, rich, poor, high caste, no caste, Muslim. For five minutes we are intensely concentrated, with a singleness of purpose, arriving, departing, haggling. Then the homogeneity melts away as the train pulls out. On one of our journeys as I haggled for oranges, lulled by childhood senses of the old steam trains whistling and huffing, I turned to discover the train sliding stealthily away and caught a glimpse of my distraught wife gesturing frantically. I made the last carriage in a sprint and it took half an hour to reach our compartment and a wife sunk in the gloom of having lost her husband on an unknown station platform. She has been your companion now for these few pages and you've caught only glimpses of her presence. Among the uniform blackness of Indian heads, her blonde hair and green eyes are quite distinctive. This shading isn't too startling in India for being the revolving door for conquerors, Indians within brown skins have the full range of blues, browns, greys, greens. Over the years, Maureen has grown more familiar with India and, quite fiercely independent, insists on making her own discoveries rather than being led by someone familiar with, and sentimental, about the history and country. Of course, she can never be a tourist in this country because of her familiarity with a family and inherited friends and acquaintances. It was easier for her than most other European wives integrating into an Indian family for we already possessed an Australian brother-in-law and the most orthodox of the family, my grand aunt, is a quietly tolerant woman. But even for her, India is not an easy country. What's it like? Her friends chorus constantly. 'Beautiful, awful, fascinating, impossible, complex,' she replies and here I am distilling a dozen dinner party dialogues, 'but it's the most challenging country I've ever been to.' (She had lived in Japan for two years and the East is familiar.) And then there are times when her patience cracks, bafflement descends, and she snaps, taking a chunk out of India for its frustrations, wastes, procrastinations. I am thankful too that Maureen holds to her own personality, resisting the temptation to dress up in a saree and, as her friends tell her, introduced Indian 'fushion' long before it ever became part of the fashion world.

On the journey, she is occupied with surreptitiously sketching our fellow passengers. Surreptitious because she is extremely shy of revealing her interest but, unnoticed by her, one of the bearers has been standing a few feet behind, totally absorbed in her drawing of the woman in our foursome. The bearer is in his mid-twenties and when he comes out to my usual post by the open window he enquires, in Tamil, whether my wife is a professional painter. 'She's learning.' He nods wisely. 'I can tell, sir. She draws and rubs out. That isn't the right way. When she draws she must do it swiftly and allow the original lines to stand. In that way only will she learn how to shape the face.' I'm not particularly surprised by his comment, only curious. 'I was an art student,' he explains. 'I studied fine arts for one year in Madras but there is no living in that, so now I work on the train.'

'I'll pass your advice on to my wife.' Quite startled, he says quickly, 'Oh no, sir, please don't tell her I said anything. It wouldn't be nice.' Only when he receives assurance does he return to his endless duties. Another time and another place, he might have lived as an artist and not worked on the Grand Trunk Express. Here and now, he is one of our millions of educated and talented who either cannot find employment or else work in menial jobs for the sake of body, if not soul. India just does not have the capacity to indulge in employment for BAs or PhDs in art, philosophy, literature, history, geography, languages. Academic positions are few and badly paid.

Dusk comes once more as the train begins to approach Jhansi, of the Rani of Jhansi fame, and if it had remained light you could have seen her fort silhouetted up in the hills. We had stayed here the previous year, 1981, for one night. To reach Jhansi it had taken us a long and exhausting day. We had begun our journey 200 miles west of Jhansi, starting at dawn in Rajasthan on the other side of the river Chambal, an ochre sluggish serpent of water. The raft that ferried us across had been a leaky, precarious vessel and reaching the Madhya Pradesh shore we'd waited an hour for a village bus at one of the remotest tea stalls in India. Also, a dangerous part of India, for we were in the Chambal ravines where India's countless dacoits raid the villages and fight gun duels with the police. One of the more glamorous dacoits, a woman named Phoolan Devi finally surrendered, not to the police, suspecting a vendetta, but to a local politician. Gradually passengers, appearing as always out of nowhere, gathered, staring at Maureen and me. They were a silent, seamed people, sinewy and resilient from the hard land and the harsh life. The chai seller gave us tea and pakodas and having broken the ice, the others approached to chat. One of the Rajasthani villagers, his head ablaze with a ponderous red turban, shyly enquired whether he could try on Maureen's shoes. For reasons beyond my male comprehension she was in pink high heels. ('Because I didn't have any flat-soled shoes. You never told me I'd end up waiting hours on a riverbank.') He tried to wiggle his foot in, failed, but still elevated himself an inch and looked as if he had scaled a minor peak. His vision of the world, after his flat-soled plastic chappals, had been transformed. When the bus finally rattled up and we clambered in, two men whom I'd not noticed earlier, both bearing ancient rifles, slid in behind us. They looked as old and worn as their weapons. I kept a nervous eye on them as hour passed hour and the bus swelled with villagers on their way to and from market with grain, vegetables, sheep, goats, pigs. A nautch woman sat beside me and her perfume was suffocating and heavy; a small girl, holding a baby goat and balancing two heavy bags of grain, was too shy to talk. Finally, the bus reached bursting capacity and the conductor winkled out all able-bodied males, except me. He quite correctly guessed that I wouldn't last too long on the roof of the bus. As the men scrambled out and on top, Maureen demanded, 'How can he treat people like that?' 'What is the villager's choice? He rides swiftly for a few pice rather than walk.' 'Why aren't there more buses?' 'They cost money, and our planners and politicians prefer to squander it on urban areas. We talk about India's strength lying in her villages but do as little as possible for them. This bus is all they have.' 'Shame!' Yes, shame, I cannot but agree. Four hours later we'd only reached Shivpur, a mere 50 miles from the Chambal. We waited another hour and another country bus took us, by night fall, to Shivpur. We reached in darkness and the mystery of India enclosed us, frightening Maureen. For the first time, she was suddenly beyond all the familiarity of the West. Here was a true India, incomprehensible to her. Jutka drivers hustled us for rides, but to where? There was nowhere here. The town was beginning to shutter up, the streets were emptying, the evening had turned chill. I was enjoying this lostness but Maureen turned grimly quiet, worrying suddenly like a child in a dark house that has in her imagination become strange and menacing. I did understand her emotion. It is that sudden moment when the world turns hallucinatory, the familiar turns alien and you wonder whether here you will die alone and unknown.

It happened to me, once. I was in the car with Arthur and Alma Standford, the subjects of my non-fiction book *Goin' Home, A Black Family Returns South.* Thames Television also made a documentary on them, along with two others I wrote for the '*Only an America*' trilogy. Arthur, a gentle, slim man, was driving. Alma, a more fiery personality, was beside him. I sat at the back. We had started from Eufaula, Alabama and were going to visit Alma's family near Tupelo, Mississippi. Tupelo had a reputation for lynching black people, even up to the 1950s. We were in 1979, so the memories were still fresh for them.

The road was lonely; it was getting dark and Alma was worried, almost in a panic. The car was low on gas. She was angry Arthur hadn't filled the tank. The car wouldn't make it to Alma's home. The trees on either side had vines hanging down, like lynch ropes, I thought. There was a weak glow of light ahead, not bright and welcoming, more menacing in this night. It was a gas station with a single pump. Beyond the pump was a room, with even dimmer lights. Arthur didn't want to stop; Alma insisted. Nervously, Arthur pulled up at the pump. The silence was broken only by crickets. Arthur didn't get out. Both turned to me. 'Will you fill up, please?' they said. 'Why?' Alma said, 'We're afraid. Nothing will happen to you, you're not black.' In this darkness, I doubted anyone could tell the difference. I got out. Still very quiet. Barely light to see the gauge as I filled the tank. The room was quiet too, no movement inside, yet I felt watched. I moved to the door to pay. As I reached it, it flew open and two white men, fighting and cursing, tumbled out. I jumped away as they both fell on the gravel. Still fighting. The door remained open and I walked in. It was a bar, four or five white men, bigger than me, sat on stools. I distracted them from the fight. They stared at me. In a movie, a freeze frame. I understood in that instant Arthur and Alma's fear. It rippled through me too. The past is too near in this lonely place. 'How many gallons?' The bartender asked. I emphasized my British accent and paid the money. And backed out, still watched. Curious, not hostile, but I still felt afraid. I knew the stories, the sudden burst of violence emphasized the danger. The two fighters had come to amicable terms and we crossed. The door closed.

I comforted Maureen, knowing it was also the exhaustion of travel. India can never frighten me. I suppose that is the definition, for me, of home. I wanted to spend the night—there was a hotel by the bus station—but Maureen wanted to move on, to escape this strange feeling invading her. I also know India in other ways. Even in this small place, there would be someone to fix our escape. With the help of a jutka driver, we ended up sitting wearily on a bench in a tiny restaurant. The cashier sent off for his boss and soon a portly, courteous man appeared by our side. He had a car that could take us to Jhansi and we agreed the price. Jhansi was only an hour away and the narrow road became a blur as our driver jousted with lorries and trucks to get us there and get back before, for him too, the night turned dangerous with dacoits, rakshashas and whatever we have invented to scare ourselves.

Jhansi then was sanctuary. Now it is a station passed in the night.

Delhi

At precisely 6.15 a.m., the Grand Trunk Express slides into New Delhi station. The ticket collector had prophesied our exact time: 'Because of its age, sir,' he told me, 'so many years it has been running, that we have a reserved platform in New Delhi station. The Grand Trunk Express never has to wait. Lesser trains have to wait many hours before they get a platform.'

We are staying with a friend of ours from New York. His house is in the southern suburb of Kailash and we putter to his home by autorickshaw over splendid three-lane highways and broad, tree-lined avenues. These monuments of the 20th century shiver and shake what remains of the city's 2000-year past. When Alexander battled the Indian king Porus, and struck a coin with their profiles on either side to honour a worthy foe, Delhi was a mud settlement. And when Caesar ruled Rome, Delhi was known as Indraprastha. No one knows when mud turned to brick and when the name changed but here Delhis lie on Delhis. The skeletons of a dozen empires are scattered in and around this city: a wall here, a tomb there, a palace here, a pillar there. New Delhi was built by our last emperor, King George V, who visited the old city in 1911 and deemed it unworthy for an imperial capital. Edward Lutyens designed this new Delhi on a grand and imperial scale and construction was finally completed in 1931. Naturally Lutyens did not consult our Shastras on how a city should be built. His model was Paris, a central pivot with spokes of avenues. The Rishis who wrote detailed instructions on how to construct our city back in the 5th century AD in the *Manasar Shilpashastras* would be horrified to see New Delhi. They would enquire: how would you defend this place? How can the evening breeze cool the town? Where is there place for the bodhi tree? And countless other questions. But they designed cities for people in the thousands, not millions.

I am impatient to continue on our journey to discover Arjumand. While Maureen rests, I rush off to the Lal Qila for the day. It stands on the banks of the Jamuna (the river distant now and fading from view) and was built between 1639 and 1648 by Arjumand's husband, the emperor Shah Jahan. Old Delhi, crowded and chaotic, narrow lanes and bazaars, bustles around the fort as it has done for four centuries. It is here that those old empires once stood and if we could but look deep into the earth, we would see the rivers of blood that have flowed through these narrow lanes. It has been sacked and re-sacked countless times, including by Timur-i-Leng, called the Scourge of God for razing cities and slaughtering the inhabitants. And then on the 10th of March 1739, the city's inhabitants attacked the men of the Persian invader, Nadir Shah. On the 11th he ordered a massacre and from dawn until midday, his army hacked to death nearly 30,000 people. The weak Mughal emperor Muhammed Shah begged for mercy, and the Persian king complied with his request, stating sarcastically: 'The Emperor of India must never ask in vain.'

Now tourists throng the Lal Qila, gazing upon history without comprehending the huge past that has accumulated in the very air of this ancient fortress. Imagine imperial soldiers, dressed in the scarlet of the great Mughals, guarding the entrance and within the courtyard, before we enter the tunnel that leads us into the garden, where the Ahadi, the emperor's personal bodyguard, inspected and searched all who entered. The captain would sit on the raised platform and every four hours, to the beating of drums and the blowing of horns, they would change the guard. Now it is a souvenir bazaar. Though I am grateful that our conquerors left us some token of the past, what has been lost is absolutely immeasurable. Nadir Shah is said to have loaded thousands of elephants and camels with the loot of Delhi, including Shah Jahan's peacock throne (which was broken up). Others came too, and what they did not carry away, they destroyed. The English were no different. They razed a great deal of the interior of this fort, leaving only Shah Jahan's palace for us to wonder at. The past, not only here but everywhere in the world, comes down to us in fragments, bits of a puzzle we try to piece together. There are many foreign tourists but most are Indian and their faces are like the shards of a mirror reflecting our past: Mongols, Persians, Turks, Greeks, Afghans, English, Portuguese, Arabs. A confusion of genes, a confusion of invasions are captured in their features; a kind of immortality does exist, filtered down through centuries. Moving through them I wonder who here is a descendant of Arjumand, who of Timur-i-Leng, who of...

Before I can go further, I have to climb up the battlement of the Delhi Gate. It is bare earth above the red sandstone; beaten, flattened and worn. I can look over the maidan to the Moti Masjid, the crowded Chandni Chowk and beyond, quite hazy, Delhis old and new. It was from here that Nehru, on the midnight of August 14th 1947, raised the Indian flag and lowered the British one. He spoke eloquently of our future: 'Long years ago we made a tryst with destiny, and now the time comes when we shall redeem our pledge. At the stroke of the midnight hour, while the world sleeps, India will awake to life and freedom. A moment comes, which comes but rarely in history, when we step out from the old to the new, when an age ends, and when the soul of a nation, long suppressed, finds utterance…'

Here too, many centuries back, was enacted another moment in history. When Shah Jahan fell ill, he crowned his eldest son Dara Shukoh as his successor. But Aurangzeb rebelled and fought two battles with Dara, and Dara lost both. In 1658 Arjumand's son, the emperor Aurangzeb, stood and watched while his elder brother Dara, Arjumand and Shah Jahan's favourite, was paraded, bound in chains, wearing torn and filthy clothes, through the streets of Delhi atop a diseased elephant. Delhi mourned for Dara and the citizens threw stones and cowdung at the man who followed him on a richly caparisoned elephant. Malik Jivan, an Afghan prince, had betrayed Dara and delivered him to Aurangzeb. His sister Jahanara, who was in Agra with her father, raced to Delhi to stop one brother killing another. She pleaded with Aurangzeb to spare Dara. Her cries fell on deaf ears.

The victor Aurangzeb, after this gloating parade, realizing

the populace was unhappy, had Dara taken down into the dungeons of the fort. There, out of sight, Dara was executed. Aurangzeb did not sign the execution warrant, he had a mullah do that for him. Like a Pontius Pilate he figuratively washed his hands, and his conscience, of killing his brother. He had another brother, Shah Shuja, assassinated and the youngest one, Murad, imprisoned for life. So, of all the four sons born to Arjumand, only Aurangzeb remained alive, fulfilling that fatal Mughal proverb: Takht ya Takhta? Throne or Coffin?

I linger on the battlement a moment longer, before descending. When the Mughal empire finally crumbled in 1857 and the British banished the 'emperor' to Burma, their army took over the fort as an encampment. Today, the Indian army occupies most of the area. My father, once an officer in that army, was posted here and told me, 'There is a stairwell beneath the palace and once as I passed through I felt an immense cold. I believe what touched me were the spirits of all those who were murdered down there.'

Above the gate and the turnstile leading into the palace grounds, once the barracks of the Ahadi, is a small, deserted museum. I'm hoping to find some trace of Arjumand or Shah Jahan here. Nothing. The only other people wandering through are a hill tribe family peering at the rusting weapons, shamshirs and khandas, patas and jamadas, shields and ancient muskets, drums and horns.

Of course the main attraction in the fort is the beautiful marble palace built by Shah Jahan. It glistens in the bright sunlight like icing on a red cake. Here the emperor held his private audiences or listened to his entertainers or dallied with his women. But every action must have dripped with the sad memory of a love who never lived to set foot within these decorated marble walls. Arjumand did not lie by the cool stream of the water that flowed through these marble pavilions, nor peer out of the intricately carved jali from the harem at her husband in the Diwan-i-Khas. Nor did she stroll along the paths through his beautiful gardens or dip her fingers in the waters of the fountain. She had died nine years before he even began to build this palace. There is nothing here for me to identify with Arjumand. Although it was within these rooms that Shah Jahan, still sexually energetic, took an aphrodisiac and fell seriously ill. The potion affected his urine tract and he lay in pain for three days and nights, and the empire slipped out of his grasp.

The Mughal emperors had acute artistic taste. They patronized architects, singers, musicians, artists, historians, poets. Within the fort, they had huge ateliers in which painters from all corners of the land executed delicate portraits of daily court life. Most of these paintings have quietly flowed abroad, ending up in the homes of our ex-rulers or else on the auction blocks of Christie's and Sotheby's. A few, however, still remain, doubtless the ones not considered the best, in the National Museum in Delhi.

On my way to the museum, I circle the Indian Parliament house. It is a great and impressive round building that blends into the patchwork of monuments in the city. I have dismal memories of my meetings with our politicians—hollow venal men, visually chaste in their white khadi, but dark and dank within. I recall interviewing a minister, not in Parliament house, but in those imperial buildings nearby that house the bureaucrats of modern India. The minister had been at Oxford with my father and this introduction wafted me down endless corridors to his palatial office. He sat, walrus-like, behind a desk and answered my journalistic queries with scant interest. He had been in power so long, fifteen years in one capacity or another, that he had become mummified in thought and action. I remember he wore a white Gandhi cap and then when tea was served on a side table in front of sofas, he removed his hat, stood up, placed a different, darker one on his head, and presided over the tea. When he returned to his desk, the reverse action took place. I knew then that this symbolism was just too obvious for me to even mention in my article. If I found him tragically amusing (he was then considered a man of great integrity though we all openly knew different) the ones now, Indira Gandhi's chamchas parading as ministers, have a suicidal effect on my mental system. They behave like princes of modern India, flowing round the country in massive and expensive entourages, and on the stump they appeal for votes to our sense of communalism. They've divided and milked us for these thirty years and I suppose we deserve every one of them because we make no protest. We reveal no moral outrage even when they are hauled to the courts and wriggle away to continue in their old ways. Their contempt for us as a people is certainly deserved. A recent study by an American Indologist, Harold A. Gould, revealed that each and every one of our countless politicians makes, even with a brief five-year term in office, enough wealth for three generations of his family. And friends too, no doubt.

The National Museum on Janpath is a large, officious-looking place guarded by an armed policeman. The cavernous interior is pretty deserted and the walls depressingly bare. The indolence of the soldier is a part of this atmosphere, the air feels lost in an eternal doze. I hunt the back corridors for the curator of Mughal miniatures and find him tucked away behind shelves of books. Mr Desai, a small, quiet man with spectacles, sits behind a huge desk, a further barricade, and blinks contemplatively at my questions. He can tell me little about Arjumand and is just barely informed about those times and those clothes. Maybe I expect too much from him and he waves with a dry hand to the books behind us. 'The best paintings are all out of the country,' he says softly, confirming my belief. 'But if you wish to find out further you may read those books.' He appears resigned to his anonymity, secure forever, until retirement carries him eventually onto the funeral pyre.

Here is the only painting of Arjumand. I stand in front of it, staring, examining every feature in the hope I can pierce the one dimension of this portrait. In this she is shown as a pretty, wide-eyed young woman with an oval face. On her head is an elaborate hat, Napoleoanic in shape though embroidered with precious stones. She has curved, well-defined eyebrows and a half-smiling mouth. Two plaits frame her face and it seems she holds a flower against her cheek. (*With the romantic imagination of a novelist I may fashion this flower into a rose of gold and emeralds, rubies and diamonds, a gift from her lover Shah Jahan.*) Her costume, neck down, is elaborate too. You cannot tell from this delicate painting how this woman could have captivated the prince Shah Jahan. In my novel, I will have to give her qualities—a voice, laughter, tears, humour, sensuality—that cannot be seen in this somewhat dull portrait. It isn't necessary that this is an accurate likeness of Arjumand. The painters were all male and none were ever permitted to look on a Mughal woman, and less so on an empress. They painted what they thought she looked like and this painting is the imagining of an artist. Yet, this woman had something very special for Khurram, the crown prince, to fall in love with her. What did he see in her that I cannot perceive in this portrait?

Agra

The next morning, Maureen and I take an Ambassador car to Agra. It is a battered vehicle, coaxed along by a burly Sikh driver. The Grand Trunk road between Delhi and Agra, a millennium old, winds through great fields of wheat stretched out to the horizon, over canals rich with water, past countless farmers bouncing along in their tractors. The road, a two-lane highway, for want of a better word, is badly maintained. Buses, lorries, cars and bullock carts jostle for space. Our Ambassador strains to overtake whenever the driver finds space. For the Amby, 0 to 60 takes at least five minutes and he never does satisfy his desire to be king of this broken road.

I feel envious of the north. In the south, we have no such riches, no largesse of water, nor the proximity of political power. The British first built these canals that vein Punjab as a reward to the Sikhs and Punjabis for enlisting in the army to fight in their endless wars, here and abroad. Now, with modern fertilizers and mechanical equipment introduced in the 1960s as part of the 'Green Revolution' of agriculture, that wealth has only multiplied. In the south, the farmer was given no such gift. He also lacks the great rivers and his state governments, ballooning with rhetoric, have never gotten round to digging him canals. They crush him under a mound of promises. In India a few miles can separate centuries. Mathura is a small town, partly populated by the army, partly too by the workers in the modern oil refinery. The metallic tubes and tanks and valves and pipes, richly silvered, dominate the skyline and the yellow smoke seeping from those high stacks drifts languidly 40 miles south to settle on the Taj Mahal.

Languidly too, centuries ago, a Persian adventurer drifted towards Agra with his wife and two small children. He was Ghiyas Beg, the future grandfather of Arjumand. In India, where romance has more appeal than harsh reality, Ghiyas Beg is supposed to have been robbed on the way, and arrived penniless in India with his wife and two children. He had abandoned the younger child, a baby girl, in the desert but a camel caravan found it and the owner of the caravan re-united the baby with its seemingly indifferent parents. The caravan owner brought the Beg family further luck. He knew the Mughal Emperor Akbar and introduced Ghiyas Beg to him. Is this fact? I'm not sure. History, as I am to gradually discover as I excavate a shard of our past, is either gossip fashioned into fact, or worse, outright distortion. Records, parchment, papyrus, clay have long returned to dust and those fragments that remained were deliberately misinterpreted by early British historians. If the Persian Ghiyas Beg's romantic life does unravel under close examination (he was sacked by Akbar for being 'too bold in taking bribes'), Akbar does not. Even through the jaundiced prism of the English eye, Akbar remained 'The Great'. The historian Sir Percival Spear brackets Akbar with the only two other 'greats' in world history, Alexander of Greece and Peter of Russia. Akbar inherited a fragmented kingdom from his highly emotional and romantic father Humayun, the son of the founder of the Mughal dynasty, Babur. In those days children were even more precocious than our 20th-century pop stars. Babur was fourteen when he began his conquests, Akbar was only thirteen when he became emperor of this almost non-existent empire and began his conquests that brought all of northern India under his control. When he was not conquering, he was marrying or concubining. In order to consolidate his kingdom, he married the daughters or sisters of princes and nobles he had defeated. He ended up with 400 wives and 5000 concubines. He was a complex man: a warrior, a mystic, an administrator, a builder, and the founder of a new religion—an amalgam of all those he saw in India—and considered himself, one isn't sure how deeply, a god. 'Allahu Akbar', the Muslim call to prayer, means 'God is Great', and Akbar seems to have thought he was, too.

He ruled India for forty-nine years and one of his legacies is our bureaucracy. Four hundred years of serpentine minds have fashioned it into its present labyrinth. It is based on the simplest philosophy: distrust. The government presumes the ulterior motives of its people, and the people in turn become ulterior in dealing with their government. I do not know which came first. Akbar, admittedly, inherited the system from Sher Shah, a Bengal king who briefly overthrew Akbar's father and in that short span of time created the complexity of our administrative system. Akbar fine-tuned it; the British tuned it finer still; the present government hones it. It was all—the mounds of paperwork, signatures upon signatures, authorization upon authorization—meant to stop corruption, but because of its maze only fosters it.

Agra then was the capital of an empire that stretched from the Himalayas down south to the Deccan and from the Persian border to Bengal. According to European travellers like Niccolao Manucci, 'Agra was larger than Rome.' Manucci, an Italian, known now as the Pepys of Mughal India came to the country at a critical point of time: the fall of Shah Jahan. His memoirs make light and interesting reading, and he writes in detail about the gossip and the events of those times. People from all over Asia, and even Europe, adventurers looking to serve one prince or another, crowded these streets. It was also on the Silk Route, and camel trains must have halted here before moving on East or West.

Arjumand would have grown up in a large house—in India things change very little for the fortunate—set in a garden. It would have been two storeys, the zenana on the second floor. She would have led a sheltered, even bland life. The daughters of noblemen learn reading and writing, painting, poetry, history and the Quran. She probably learned to ride too, for polo was then popular among the ladies of the court. Maybe she even handled a musket as women also accompanied men on shikars. Today a girl will go to university and get a degree but this education is often merely to increase her value in the marriage market: 'Educated girl, fair complexion ...'

Life then, as long as Akbar was in residence (rarely) was centred around the Agra Lal Qila. His wives and concubines and other members of his family lived in mansions or the red sandstone palace within the fort. Akbar himself lived in a massive and elaborate tent, richly decorated, pitched on the lawn outside the palace. Timur-i-Leng had decreed that none of his descendants must sleep under a fixed roof; a reminder of their nomadic inheritance; and the Mughal emperors obeyed this decree. Of course, the Bargah was a splendid tent: two floors, its interior walls lined with silk or else covered with paintings, the ground soft with Persian and Kashmiri carpets. While on the move—which was often as they were all nomadic at heart—the emperors lived in the Do-ashiyana manzils which had enough room even for their harems.

We too, in far less ostentatious nomadism, spent part of our childhood in tents as we wandered India. They were simple ones: a couple of rooms to sleep in with tables set outside for meals. As children we took great delight in this spare existence. At night, the wind stroked the canvas walls and the lamp light flickered, hurling black shapes over our heads and when we woke at dawn, we found that the dew had crept in and the grass was cold and damp. We spent part of a summer in one on a farm in Hosur, a village near Bangalore. The tent stood on the lawn which was bordered with jagged tin teeth that discouraged snakes from invading our privacy. However, one afternoon Sheba, our mongrel dog, stampeded a herd of cattle across the lawn and demolished tent, crockery, bedding and books. Naturally we children were blamed for this act of destruction. This fragment of memory fades as we pass the hawkers outside the Lal Qila and enter the fort. Arjumand, her family and other nobles would have entered the fort through the

Amar Singh Darwaza. The Delhi Darwaza and the Hathi Pol Darwaza were exclusively for the Mughal army which occupied half the fort. She would have passed imperial soldiers in scarlet uniforms, armed with swords and shields. The fort is shaped like a bow, with the 'string' facing the river.

The road slopes steeply upwards and we find ourselves in the palace garden where the magnificent tent was once pitched. This fort too once blazed with life—the Meena Bazaar selling everything from fresh vegetables to gold and silks, offices for the bureaucracy, barracks for the Imperial army and, beyond the palace, the stables for the horses and elephants and menageries of wild beasts. It would have been crowded with nobles and countless women, some wives, and others, as Roe described, 'whoores'.

The guides hustling the tourists are totally ignorant but even their banal lies cannot diminish the splendour of the Mughal palace. The marble chambers built by Shah Jahan are silken and cool to our touch and the inlaid floral designs (leaf and vegetable dye) leap out of the stone. All this wasn't built when Arjumand was a child and only briefly, as the Empress, did she experience the splendour, and this after four years of hardship and privation spent fleeing from her father-in-law and Mehrunissa's wrath.

But what we see of the palace is only the surface. Below are six more floors, locked and barred, which I want to explore. I am told to obtain permission from the archeological office on the Mall (A favorite street name for a different empire). It is a single-storey bungalow, crowded with desks, files, clerks, officials, peons; a slumberous sort of place, awash with paper. I expect the usual problems dealing with our bureaucracy but to my surprise, a young assistant curator casually waves aside formality. We can view the lower floors that afternoon if we wish. You can never make any presumptions with Indian officialdom. A much lower functionary, the keeper of the fort's keys, Mohan Das, a man in his thirties, neatly dressed in a bush shirt, pressed slacks and chappals, awaits us in the guard room at three o'clock. He has indeed received orders to open up whatever I want. He gathers up a torch and a ring of heavy keys, and leads us to the palace. There is a barred door set under the Machchi Bhawan, hidden by bushes and he opens it with a flourish. The air beneath the palace has a cool, musty odour, stirring memory, but I can't place the smell. The walls down here are not of marble, but plaster, smooth and polished, an art now forgotten in India. So much has been forgotten and we re-acquire these skills as if they are new inventions. The floors are covered with three or four inches of fine dust.

'These first rooms were dungeons for the ladies,' Mohan Das says. 'They were imprisoned here for a day or two, a most mild punishment.'

I am unsure whether to believe him—so much has been forgotten. However, I am sure, as we pass through the gloomy corridors and arched chambers, that this was once the repository of the fabulous Mughal treasury. The treasury was directly beneath the harem, and was guarded by three rings of soldiers. The outer ring consisted of men: the Emperor's Ahadi; the centre ring of Tartar women slaves, fierce warriors; the inner ring of eunuchs. What they guarded was incalculable: tubs of diamonds, emeralds, rubies, pearls, gold coins, silver coins, gold thrones, gold saddles, gold howdahs, gold chairs, silver tables. When the empire fell, the plunderers swarmed down into these rooms. The Mughals were the richest kings in the world. On Akbar's death, historians have calculated that he left in cash alone, ignoring diamonds, gold and other priceless knick-knacks, 24 million pounds sterling. It certainly needed the thousand camels and elephants to carry this plunder back to the Persian kingdom of Nadir Shah.

(There is a small cavity by the wall outside the Diwan-i-Aam which the guides point to as the treasury of the Mughals. How can they possibly imagine the physical space needed for the fabulous wealth of the Great Mughal? Certainly money was stored out there in the open. Leather bags of rupees and dams were filled daily and distributed to the poor as alms.)

Descending further into greater darkness, the chill increases. The odour suddenly springs to life. A million bats cling to the walls down here, and the torchlight ripples over their shiny black skins and, as they hurl themselves in flight, reflects on tiny ruby eyes. Maureen screams and clings to me but Mohan Das and I are quite unsympathetic to this fear. Bats, I lecture as they squeak and fill the small rooms with the whoosh of their countless wings, have excellent sonar and will not collide with us. This is meagre comfort but she bravely trudges behind us, ducking and weaving. There is a balcony on the third floor down, and before it a marble bath. Prisoners were allowed to bathe and then stand on the balcony to see their relatives across the fort's wall. Another chamber, very gloomy, is supposedly the execution room. The prisoners here were ordinary felons; the princely rascals were held in the Gwalior fort, 200 miles south. I want to go further down, down to the very bottom. 'Snakes,' Mohan Das says laconically, and we are immediately discouraged. I grew up in a garden filled with cobras and have a greater respect for their bad temper than for hysterical bats. Reluctantly I return back up into the sunlight and surreptitiously drag my feet through the fine dust. Maybe the plunderers dropped a ruby or a diamond but all I come up with are dusty toes.

On the way back, Mohan Das tells us that some years ago a couple of these floors were open to the public. One day the chowkidar smelt a bad odour and a search revealed a murdered man. He had been there a few weeks and with that deep suspicion authority here harbours for the people, they closed the rooms forever. Who knows? It could have become a popular locale for more murders: deep and dark and murky, hidden from sunlight within the cold walls that have witnessed countless executions.

Mohan Das says they never did solve the case nor discover the identity of the dead man. Revealing this secret, this tidbit of gore which remains hidden from the hoi-poloi milling around on the marble terraces, makes Mohan Das now quite magnanimous. He wishes to reveal further secrets, open further doors. He jangles his keys, like the vizier of an emperor, and leads us back up into the sunlight and the air loses its sense of intrigue, deaths and priceless riches.

'Come,' he whispers, moving towards a locked room across the terrace.

We enter a bare rectangular chamber with polished plaster walls, faintly decorated with flowers. This is the bathing chamber of the emperor and empress. I cannot suppress lascivious imagination here. Arjumand revealed: the beautiful body dewed with water, drops clinging to her breasts, glistening on her flanks. You must depend on my imagination; no one ever saw her naked except Shah Jahan and the female slaves gently washing that soft ivory-coloured skin, caressing that breathing sensual flesh. Dried, perfumed, and then, like a portcullis falling, the veil draped her from head to toe and she retreated into mystery: hidden for another day, hidden forever.

Beyond this bath is an ante-chamber. A small window frames the Taj Mahal in the distance, like a Mughal miniature. The light is hazy with pollution though. A raised platform runs along the wall, and a precisely circular hole has been made in the centre of the floor.

'Eighty feet,' Mohan Das says, and points to it. 'See how clever they were. No smells.'

I peer down to where the imperial shit fell on the rocks. Beside the stones is a small opening in the fort's wall. The shit could not have remained there for ever. Through the opening, an untouchable, trapped in the eternity of his caste, would have washed down those stinking rocks. Even these rooms are always closed to the public for, elevating themselves to imperial stature, they too could use this as their toilet. 'Dirty people,' Mohan Das says with imperial contempt.

There is more. More locks, more doors. The Moti Masjid, the Pearl Mosque, built by Shah Jahan, standing at the north-west corner of the palace grounds, is locked too. But Mohan Das jangles his keys as we cross the gardens. Intimates now in our secrets, Mohan Das confesses he has a lowly position, a wife, three children, he has passed the bureaucratic exams for promotion but the third cousin of a superior, a man with no qualifications, no family to support, an upstart, an ignorant idiot, now has the job my friend Mohan Das coveted. Ahhh, but it is such a common complaint in India. We are a people of cousins, first, second, third, fourth, fifth, and cousins of cousins, all gripping fiercely to our backs if we happen to be in a position to grant the favour of nepotism. Mohan Das understands his superior. His sigh of longing tells me this. We are trapped by the burden of this past, the collusions of Hindu, Muslim, Sikh, Parsi, Brahmin, Sudra, Tamil, Punjabi, castes, communities, tribes, family, atoms splitting into selfish loyalties. It suffocates our dreams, crushes hope. We grow lethargic, fatalistic, pinioned forever by these intangible claws. Mohan Das accepts grumbling defeat, still dreaming of escape. Where? Away, away from the past, from identity. He sighs for the Middle East, longs for America. To be unknown, to rise on ability, free from superiors' cousins, free from his caste. We have political freedom but not the deeper, richer one that will allow us to float away from our cursed identities. But I know, as he knows: if the roles were reversed, Mohan Das would behave exactly in the same manner as his superior.

Escape is illusion. I return eagerly to my past, as do other Indians: from the Middle East, Singapore, Hong Kong, England and the United States, wherever we have scattered. And on return, helplessly revert: mother India smothers us in her coils. A return feels like a film run backwards at tremendous speed. Actions, thoughts, experience, even age, are undone. I become Indian (and I wish it to stop here but it is unstoppable) Hindu, Madrasi, caste, son of so-and-so, grandson of... I am re-enclosed in the womb; the mucous of my antecedents clings to me even now as I travel north. We can, with a glance, classify faces, names, dress, tongue, food, worship; and condemn or condone. Even metaphysically we are haunted: the past of different lives and different acts leads us circuitously into this present moment of action. I cannot shake off the despair for ourselves as I listen to Mohan Das.

There is no escape from this karma which sprang its trap for Arjumand. She was twelve years old when, here within these walls, she saw Prince Khurram, son of Jahangir, the Great Mughal. With a snap of fate, they fell in love at the Royal Meena Bazaar.

Imagine the month of May and the dry, searing, suffocating heat. It is night and the garden is ablaze with lights. The still air is perfumed with sandalwood and rose and jasmine, filled too with the sweet sounds of music and the excited laughter of women. Stalls have been erected and the grassy lanes between them covered with Persian carpets. This is the night of the Royal Meena Bazaar. The one night in the year when the ladies of the court may appear naked faced in front of specially invited nobles, and behave in the bawdy, swaggering manner of the low-class bazaar women for whom such facial freedom is taken for granted.

One of the special invitees was the prince, Khurram, son of the Mughal Emperor Jahangir, Padshah of Hindustan. Khurram must have been around fifteen years old and the invitation signalled that his presence at the Royal Meena Bazaar was a sign of not only his father's favour but also of the other court nobles. It elevated him above his brothers,

Khusrau, Parviz and Shahriyar. For Khurram this was to be a fortuitous event as it confirmed he was the heir to the Mughal Empire and he must have strutted in, not expecting to also be gifted with falling in love.

Arjumand's stall, I imagine, is hidden in a far corner, and she sits cross-legged in front of an insignificant handful of silver jewellery. She is twelve and unimportant. Her grandfather, Ghiyas Beg, no longer works for the Great Mughal. Akbar has been dead for two years and Jahangir is yet to employ the Persian. Arjumand is shy and beautiful and alive with curiosity, openly amused by this great tamasha, looking at the magnificent wares the other women have come to sell. Gold, precious stones, ivory, silks. They flirt and giggle, and flatter the passing Emperor Jahangir, trailed by his nobles. Arjumand's aunt Mehrunissa also has her own stall selling her designer outfits. Jahangir sees her, and that is the start of that affair which ends in marriage and Mehrunissa becomes Nur Jahan. Prince Khurram would have entered later, after his father had left, surrounded by his acolytes. He strolls here and there, enticed by the women: some beautiful, others not, young and old, from every land, eager to receive his favours, lusting for the power he will one day command. And then by chance, he stops, turns and sees Arjumand. And she, him. They must have talked, touched and then Khurram would have left, leaving behind Arjumand who must have wondered what might happen next. The other women, including Mehrunissa, would have noticed this exchange and dismissed it as a prince's passing fancy...

Looking down on the garden from the height of the Moti Masjid through the haze of 377 years, we can believe that love-at-first-sight is not a 20th-century discovery. Shah Jahan fell instantaneously, head-over-heels in love. The moment froze, the world slid away, love engulfed them both. The stuff of romantic novelists, the songs of poets over centuries, the dreams of youths and maidens. A prince of the empire smitten by a slight girl of twelve. And she by him. Who truly knows what he saw? It was sheer chance, karma, the stars in conjunction, the moon rising, the sun falling, whatever, that he saw her naked face. What luck! To step but once from behind the 'wall of chastity' and love strikes. Was she beautiful? We must believe, we must fantasize that Arjumand's face stopped the hearts of men. Grey eyes, maybe brown, liquid, serene, sparkling; a sensual mouth plucked from the faces of those voluptuous goddesses carved on the temples of Khajuraho whose sexuality vibrates down through eleven centuries; high cheekbones, an oval face, or was it? This is fantasy. She can be shaped to fit any imagination for we are not restrained by a true likeness. What did they speak of then when they surfaced back to that night and the jostle of courtiers, the laughter and shouting? A fragment, supposedly accurate, remains. Khurram: How much are your wares? Arjumand: All of them? Khurram: Yes. Arjumand (laughing): Ten thousand rupees, Your Highness. Khurram: I will l pay it.

Bland. Certainly not immortal. What then? Our gossip columnist, our court reporter, standing at the shoulder of this Mughal prince has an attack of amnesia. He does not report whether the prince utters, 'I love you' or that Arjumand replies, 'I love you too.' Nothing about the collision of planets, the will of Allah, a besotted prince mooning and whispering her name: Arjumand, Arjumand. Of course, our scribe was not to know how momentous this mundane commercial transaction was to be. If he had stood at my vantage point twenty-five years after that encounter, he would have seen the Taj Mahal rising in the distance. Out of a 10,000-rupee bargain sprang the most beautiful monument on earth.

On the opposite side of the Moti Masjid are low, ugly army barracks. Mohan Das nervously requests me to hide the camera. A couple of Jawans glance up, indifferent to the camera. The Indian government prohibits photographing military installations and airports. To another side of the mosque is something that looks like a dried riverbed, flanked by broken buildings. This was once the real Meena Bazaar. Mohan Das has exhausted his secrets, much to his own chagrin, and re-locks the mosque's ancient doors. Tourists make a rush but he shoos them away, and we follow him back to the entrance of the Lal Qila. He waves aside my tip and disappears into a dark cubbyhole with his precious keys.

In Agra you find yourself adopted by cycle rickshawwallahs. There is no escaping their persistence or patience: once you have sat in their vehicles, you are their property for the length of your stay. No excuse is acceptable and now our man, having waited hours, hurries over to usher us back into his care. We ride the narrow road along the Jamuna, with the fort to our left. Once it must have been an awesome spectacle: the walls manned by imperial guards and the maidan between the walls and the river crowded with events: elephant fights, executions, strolling magicians, petitioners awaiting a glimpse of the Great Mughal at the Jarokha-i-Darshan.

The river's life remains unchanged. It has a sense of eternal continuity: boys playing and rising, brown skins silvery with water, buffaloes wallowing, women beating clothes, drying them on the sand, a neat field of rushes planted in a small impermanent sandy island. It would have been the same then. Each time the water rose, washing away life, life returned, persistent, blindly optimistic, forgetting the rage of this placid stream when it is swollen by the monsoons.

Behind the fort, still clinging to the walls, lies ancient Agra. Older than even the Lal Qila: a warren of houses, lanes, shops, glossed with 20th-century electricity, transistor radios, TVs, scooter repair shops. Like the river this, too, remains unchanged. The faces that slide by us, in their countless reincarnations, have seen the rise and fall of countless empires. They have suffered slaughter too, trapped here between the juggernauts of armies.

In 1657 their ancestors were conscripted into Prince Dara's army. He had already lost one battle against his brother Aurangzeb. That took place on the banks of the Chambal river. Now he makes a last-ditch effort to beat his brother. Shah Jahan has opened the treasury to finance this new army. When it marches out of Agra in the thousands, the sun glittering on lances, swords, shields, canons, muskets, Manucci describes it as a most awe-inspiring sight but, 'the army was composed mainly of the ordinary citizens of Agra, the butchers and bakers and shoe makers.' Dara lost this battle too and fled westwards and doubtless the Agra citizens immolated their dead and licked their wounds, preparing themselves for the coming of a new emperor.

Our rickshaw crosses the Jamuna bridge: a strand of iron carrying a rail line and a narrow pitted road. The rickshaw glides between bullock carts, cyclists, scooters, pedestrians. Heavier traffic is prohibited, though how this frail span can carry a train is an unpleasant thought. Half a mile south of the bridge is the tomb of the Persian adventurer Ghiyas Beg. It was built by his daughter (Arjumand's aunt) Mehrunissa, a woman who deserves a novel of her own. She married a General, captivated the Mughal emperor Jahangir, her husband the General was murdered (some say by Jahangir), married Jahangir after keeping him waiting four years, and finally became empress of India. She wrote poetry, painted, designed clothes, played polo, and shot big game. She ruled the empire from the harem and Roe, in a letter to Charles I, wrote, 'she governs him (Jahangir) and wynds him up at her pleasure.' Her pleasure too had her father reinstated in court. Doubtless Ghiyas Beg continued to be bold in taking bribes but he had her protection and a new mantle of authority, he was the I'timad-ud-daula. His tomb is pretty and small, set in a pleasant garden and quite devoid of tourists though not of guides, lounging under a tree drinking chai. It seems a pleasant place to lie. The dome is the obvious model for the Taj Mahal. The fountains here are dry and dusty and ... a young guide hustles us, 'Come, I can tell you more about this tomb than anyone else.' He grandly proclaims himself to be the caretaker and bustles around pointing out the obvious. Here there are no secrets to be revealed, only inlaid flowers and low sarcophaguses: Ghiyas Beg and his wife in one chamber, and in others his son (Arjumand's father) and Mehrunissa's daughter and her family. The whole Persian clan lies here except the two most important women. Mehrunissa lies in Lahore, while from a window our guide points, 'See from here you cannot see the red sandstone of the Taj Mahal, only the marble. Wasn't Shah Jahan clever?'

Taj Mahal

Does it not deserve to have a chapter of its own, for that is why millions visit Agra? 'Only let this one tear drop glisten spotlessly bright on the cheek of Time forever and ever,' wrote Rabindranath Tagore, the only Indian to date to have won the Nobel Prize in literature. Kipling too, another Nobel laureate, wrote on the Taj. And so did Aldous Huxley: 'Marble, I perceive, covers a multitude of sins.' And countless others. The Taj has constantly been awash in words. I will not interrupt your viewing nor reel off the statistics, the niggling details about length, breadth, the number of precious stones, the way the bricks were made. The foundation was a series of piers straddling a series of wells which would eventually be connected by strong arches. The cores of these wells would be filled with rubble, then the spaces between each with solid masonry. The piers would support the massive weight of the tomb, while the wells would prevent the river Jamuna from seeping under it...

Two hoary myths need dispelling here. The most popular of which, now fading with the passage of time and empires, is the one that the Taj Mahal was designed and built by an Italian jeweller. There were certainly a number of Europeans knocking around Agra in the 17th century.

Apart from Manucci, and Bernier and Tavernier, two French travellers, there were Portuguese and British mercenaries working for the Mughal army. Myths naturally arise from our perception of another race. The Europeans, then greedy for the fabled wealth of India, did not wish to believe that Indians could have designed and built such a magnificent monument. And what better way to promote doubt than to invent an unnamed Italian to oversee the Taj Mahal from foundation to dome. The Mughals were meticulous in their documentation, we have not only the names of the main contractors, and administrators—thirty-seven in all—Ismail Afandi, the Turkish dome builder, Chiranji Lal, the Hindu lapidarist, but also their salaries. And not an Italian name is to be found.

The true architect of the Mumtaz Mahal was Shah Jahan. He captured in marble what Da Vinci captured on canvas. The Mumtaz Mahal is his portrait of Arjumand. Her eyes, her nose, the smile on her lips, the delicacy of her cheeks, the roundness of her bosom, the calmness of her spirit. If you can but peer through the gauze of your imagination, you will see her rise before you in this marble tomb. And on a moonless night when the shadows deepen the mystery of the Taj Mahal you will hear her breathing and sighing. Shah Jahan left the world not a marble tear drop but a marble sculpture of his beautiful wife.

And then we say, did not Shah Jahan, once the tomb was completed, execute all who worked on it? Did he not cut off noses and hands and gouge out eyes? These savage acts were supposedly committed in order to prevent anyone building an imitation of the Taj Mahal. However, given the times and his awesome power, Shah Jahan was a compassionate monarch. People wept when he was overthrown by his son Aurangzeb for he was known as 'the father of his people'. Compassion aside, Shah Jahan was also a compulsive builder. He needed his talented designers, carvers, and inlayers to work on the Agra palace, the Delhi palace, the Lahore palace and those exquisite pavilions which you will soon see in Ajmer. The Mughals spent fortunes patronizing the arts. Even their dreaded ancestor, Timur-i-Leng, whom no one could accuse of artistic sensibilities, prized talented men. When he plundered India, part of his plunder was human: sculptors, musicians, painters, carpet weavers. They were rounded up and bundled off to work for him in Samarkand.

Beauty can still the destructive impulses of men. Four centuries of conquests and wars have raged around the Taj Mahal, and though the Persian and the Jat did plunder the tomb of its silver doors and inlaid precious stones, they left it relatively unharmed. They were awed by its beauty, soothed by its icy calm and took only what they thought was unnecessary. When you see the ruins of so many empires, razing being a favourite past-time of our conquerors, one can sigh in relief that the Taj survived. It even survived the destructive impulses of our British overlords, the Marquis of Hastings and Lord Bentinck. Both of them wanted to break up the tomb and sell the marble to dealers in Calcutta. Fortunately for the Taj Mahal, the marble prices in London dropped as the British had discovered porcelain for their bathrooms. Instead, they turned their mercantile impulses to Shah Jahan's Agra palace and destroyed the beautiful bathroom. It was the Viceroy, Lord Curzon, who not only saved the Taj Mahal but also carried out much needed repairs after centuries of neglect.

A long time ago, as a child, I sat in my mother's lap, surrounded by brothers and sisters and father, waiting too for the moon to rise. My father was posted to Agra and I am told we would picnic in the gardens. My eldest sister Nalini recalls the scene clearly and her words echo now as I wait here: 'It was very dark and we were huddled up against Amah. Then the light began to slowly creep in through the trees towards the Taj Mahal. Pah! It still makes me shiver. Only at night do you realize it is a tomb. It looks cold, alone and sad. I remember too, when the moon rose, looking around and seeing so many people sitting quietly.'

Now of course there is no quiet. The world is constantly awash with tourists. Chatter, chatter, chatter. Camera flashes burn the night, futilely trying to cage the vast magic of white marble, the garden, the shadow of moonlight. The greed of our visual senses cannot be captured by the miniature imagination of the camera. I note other tiny sparks: brief, brilliant. Luminescent fireflies appearing and disappearing on the lawn. I remember at home in my garden, I'd spend many twilight hours chasing these motes of light, but it has been a long time since I've seen them. I wonder where they have gone.

A young Australian comes to sit by Maureen and as they are both from the same country they drift into one of those meaningless 'where from?' conversations. He has been travelling for months and even in this gloom I note the stunned and weary stare of sight-seeing indigestion. He looks ahead at the Taj Mahal uncomprehendingly as the moonlight starts to creep through the trees. It is inching its way to the plinth of the tomb.

'Do you know anything about the Taj Mahal?' Maureen asks.

'Only what I read on the plaque outside,' he replies, unashamed of his ignorance. It is his right as a tourist to see, not comprehend. 'It's bigger than I thought it would be.'

'You should tell him,' Maureen says to me.

What can I tell this stranger about my obsession? Would he understand? I doubt it. He looks too young, too weary, skating swiftly over the surface of India.

Tell him.

'The dome is a double dome, one built on another, so you get the impression of height. It alone weighs twelve hundred tons. The height...'

What am I doing? Boring him and myself. His awe has diminished. I have reduced magnificence to statistics. How can I be so crass? The Taj is not feet and inches. It is a dream. It is about the men and women who created it for Arjumand. A man squatting in the shade of a tree painfully chipping away from a block of marble the jali that surrounds her sarcophagus. Day in and day out, year upon year, uncomprehendingly. He created that delicate, fragile screen—one of the greatest pieces of Indian sculpture—on the orders of the emperor Shah Jahan.

But let us leave the Mumtaz Mahal with the thought that having survived the crash of so many empires the tomb is now threatened, not by conquerors, but ourselves. We, an independent India, will consume the marble with our soot and ash and fumes, and have none to blame except ourselves.

On Riots

I had long planned to visit Aligarh, a town that makes the third point of a triangle between Agra and Delhi. In Aligarh is to be found the ultimate authority on the Mughal period. I had written to Irfan Habib, a radical, left-wing Mughal historian at Aligarh University, weeks ago but had received no reply. I hoped he could tell me more about Arjumand. I had tried phoning but the Indian telephone system was beyond comprehension. It functioned according to its own mystical logic and was appropriately Indian. Tantalizingly there, yet separate from our own daily need.

Aligarh is a two-hour bus ride through the rich, lush fertile plains of Uttar Pradesh and we reach the town ahead of schedule but once we enter the outskirts our bus driver turns overly cautious. We creep through empty streets. The shops everywhere are shuttered and people peer down from barred windows. I wonder if it's a holiday. In the town centre, we suddenly come upon lines of policemen. Some are on horseback, others waiting in side streets. They all wear helmets and carry lathis. They are ominously visible, yet ignored. What has happened? When you travel, you lose touch with wars, disasters, crises, political eruptions, sports, plane crashes, assassinations. You live in a suspended reality until the moment your bus drops you off in the midst of policemen who eye you suspiciously.

'What has happened? What has happened?'

No one replies. We are all ignorant. We move through the policemen—Maureen highly visible in this mass of dark people. She notes my anxiety but is serenely unaware of the madness of Indian mobs. Taxi drivers hurl themselves at us, and one, offering a ride to the university for thirty-five rupees, twice confirmed, whisks us away from the visible tension. The university is some distance from the bus station. It stretches along a quiet, gardened street. Students wander along in twos and threes, deceptively calm. They have long had the reputation themselves for riots, lockouts, gheraoes, strikes, violence. Often as not the centre of the storm is Irfan Habib, through no fault of his own.

The history department is in a modern building and I have an introduction to one of Irfan's assistants, Parvathi Menon. She turns out to be an enormously pretty girl—the kind men can fall in love with instantly. She is friendly, shy and as we get to know her, very dogmatic in her opinions.

'What's happening in town?' I ask.

My dormant reportorial instincts, like doused passion, struggle to revive their old ardour. I suspect I'm already snuffling cold ashes.

'A riot,' she says dismissively. 'There was a Holi procession and it went into the Muslim part of town. Then the fighting began and the police are trying to keep the two sides apart.'

I have been harsh about her complacency. I too lose enthusiasm. Another Hindu-Muslim riot. Another body count. Another ancient enmity aroused, and now merely checked, ticking furiously, waiting for the next spark. If that recipe should dull, the choice is boundless: Hindu-Sikh, Muslim-Sikh, Congress-Communist, Hindu-Hindu (inter-caste) north-south-east-west, management-labour. Singly we are a servile people. We bow and scrape and cringe, history has hammered at us for too long. We have a surface amiability that arises from having to compromise with gods, conquerors, employers. We exist. Another day to be negotiated in the storm of uncertainties: jobs, castes, salaries, security; yet beneath we seethe. Rage is skin deep; a powder keg of bone, muscle, blood. We drift in the tide of some slight—a cow killed, water drunk from a well, a pig thrown against a mosque—gathering anger, gathering courage, twos, threes, hundreds, thousands, and then blood and bodies shimmer in the fires. Women, children, old and young men, hacked, beaten, stabbed, and the asbestos blankets of the police (or soldiers) smother the flames for a moment.

The day was 30 January 1948 and we were at a film matinee. I cannot remember the title though Nalini tells me it was a Hindi film. I was in the company of her, Padmini, and various female cousins. Suddenly, we noticed our chauffeur peering through the darkened theatre. He saw us, hurried over and commanded, 'Come.' Even as he spoke, the film stopped and the lights came on. No one moved. The chauffeur was harshly insistent. Then a scrawl appeared on the screen, faintly discernible: 'Gandhi has been assassinated.' We rushed out. We ran not from sorrow, but fear. My grandparents expected rioting. And we all thanked god Gandhi's assassin was Hindu.

Irfan Habib is a small, shy man sitting alone in his office. He has some fame in India and as the centre of so many whirling controversies my image of him had been of someone bristling, bearded, roaring. I can hardly even hear him speak. There are rows of chairs in front of his desk. Yes, he had been expecting me, but he has to rush off to a meeting. Could I meet him later? I am only too eager to defer. I expect to be eventually told all manner of wondrous things about Arjumand.

On our way back from a hurried lunch, the taxi runs out of gas. The only pump is miles away and we decide to transfer to a cycle rickshaw. Our driver now claims he meant 350 rupees, certainly not thirty-five. After a bitter quarrel with the badmash, I part with fifty, but he continues his tirade even as we slowly fade from his sight.

Arriving late for Irfan Habib, I find I have to share him with a reporter from a Delhi magazine. She's in her twenties, very self-assured and important, and trailed by a photographer. She wants to interview Irfan on the riot and he looks a bit unsettled, but is too polite to refuse the request. So while she waits in the last row of chairs, I try to get Irfan to discuss Arjumand.

'There's not much to tell about her. Very little is known,' he shrugs. 'If you want to find out more about Mughal women, you should read this book.' A quick scrawl of a title, and then more titles. A cascade of books rains down from his pen.

I realize now I am confronting a man with too much knowledge. His mind is a great mass of information and unless I am specific—date, size, etc.—he cannot respond.

He cannot recount the court gossip about Arjumand while he can discuss agrarian reforms under Emperor Akbar. He burdens me with reading, and then I am dismissed to accommodate the reporter. He also has to attend a colleague's funeral ceremonies. I caught him on the wrong day and, disappointed, we trudge down to the library with Parvathi and two of her colleagues, a girl, Rana, and a man, Iftikhar.

They are eager to help and haul down tome upon tome for me. I have read some but in the writing of fiction, dogmatic history should be kept somewhat at bay, otherwise the imagination becomes hopelessly yoked to meandering, intricate events and a cast of thousands. I flick through the tomes. The world I have entered is dryly academic, self-contained, theoretical and I beat a retreat from this onslaught of print. Upstairs, Parvathi introduces me to other historians. They have doctorates in Mughal history and confronted by such accumulated expertise I find it surprisingly easy to chat over tea. They all appear to consult the same volumes for their research, the *Ain-i-Akbari* by Abu'l Fazl. He was Akbar the Great's official biographer and his three-part book is crammed with the minutest details of Akbar's rule. From the shape of a sword, to the rotation of crops, to the number of muskets, to the pay of the harem women. Fazl was Akbar's best friend and tragically ended up being assassinated on Jahangir's orders. I had already bought and read the *Ain-i-Akbari* and could discourse on it. However, my companions are intensely curious as to how one writes a novel on the subject. Fiction, within these walls, is frivolous.

'We live,' says one lady academic, 'such insular lives. We study the same books and each paper we write narrows our world down further and further.'

It is a sad cry, which I cannot answer. All our lives are narrow beams of thought and energy as we trudge from womb to grave. I borrow a monograph on Mughal titles and ranks before escaping. I am a diversion in their lives; and they in mine. We will return to our paths soon. Parvathi and her two friends suggest another tea break in the college tea shop. It is a little thatched hut leaning against the compound wall at the back of the history department. Here we begin a long, heated discussion on the film *Gandhi*. Parvathi insists it should have been historically accurate, containing the minutiae of his life. I cannot persuade her that a motion picture, like a novel, is only the interpretation of its creator. After cups of tea, I change the topic. I discover all three of them are on scholarships and are grimly hoping these will be extended at the end of the year. It is their only security for once it's over, they have to enter the academic world and the jobs they would like are non-existent. They look mournfully out at a life that holds little future for their talents.

Delhi Again

Awaiting the Varanasi Express to Delhi. Street dogs scavenge along the tracks, coolies squat in emaciated lines, women and children sleep, a man bathes under a tap, our lives here are so open to public scrutiny. I feel dejected. What did I expect? Hours of conversation, easy access to the secrets of Arjumand? I had wanted the book of Irfan Habib's mind open for my selection: a bit of this, a bit of that; and I have her whole. Of course, a historian cannot understand my quest. Frivolous, I think he too must think that. The stuff of novels does not inflame him; sepulchral facts do. He cannot dream of Arjumand. What thesis can support such a slight figure in history? Balanced against her are Akbar, Jahangir, Shah Jahan, Aurangzeb, the cost of grain, the price of horses, the wages of peasants. Those are honest things to write about; the stuff of Royal Societies. She was fluent in Persian and Urdu, composed poetry and gave generously to charity but beyond that there is so little written about her.

The coolies have become alert. They hurry to line up alongside the track, strategically spaced, obviously territorial. We cannot see nor hear anything. A sixth sense has aroused them—the Varanasi train comes, a half hour late. The great diesel engine throbs in and the platform is awash with life: sellers of chai, samosas, magazines, books, paan, biscuits, fruit; beggars, bedding, cases, children. It is only a short commute to Delhi but journeys anywhere are a great event, especially today as the buses have stopped plying. The drivers have no wish to be stoned by rioters.

We find an empty carriage, dusty with the long haul from the holy city, settle in, and gaze out at the landscape slowly adrift in the dusk. Arjumand passed here often, her trail crisscrossed, reclining in her carriage accompanied by horsemen, slaves, maidservants, eunuchs. But that was only when she became empress, and that is still some years off.

What happened then—you ask—after that night at the royal Meena Bazaar? Did they court and dance? Did Shah Jahan rush to his father and her father demanding marriage to this wondrous girl?

Nothing happened. Arjumand returned to the cloister of the zenana. Prince Khurram, the scoundrel, married another girl. She was a relation of the Shahenshah of Persia, and doubtless it was a political match, so I should not blame the prince. The Padshah of Hindustan and the Shahenshah were ancient foes. Their empires overlapped in Kandahar, an Afghan town buried in the past and now locked away in the Russian embrace. Then it was the portal through which the two empires viewed one another. A prince of one marrying a princess of the other was diplomatic common sense. Did not Akbar take 400 wives, and 5000 concubines out of diplomatic necessity? The palace was flooded with women. Women, women. The artefacts for an emperor, smothered in luxury, pampered, unused, rusting in their loins for only one man was permitted to lie with them.

Arjumand mourned, hurt. What chance had she now to marry Khurram? She could have become his second wife or his third. I believe she refused. She would be first or nothing. But she was no princess, there was no diplomatic necessity, no wealth. Wealth? How could a Persian adventurer's granddaughter ever match the stupendous riches of the Great Mughal? Brooding in that long claustrophobic room, peering through the latticed windows out into the garden or through the myopic gauze of her veil, she must have ceased hoping. That love at first sight had been a cruel illusion, a trick played upon her heart, now hammering hopelessly within her breast. The ash of despair must have been bitter in her young mouth. But do not give up hope for our heroine. Her life was never easy. It was as torturous as the path we have to follow to discover her.

We have halted now at the outskirts of Delhi. We can see the lights of the great ring road and the colonies of houses that make up the suburbs of this city. Tantalizingly near but still hours away as the train probes and prods forward. This is not the Grand Trunk Express and there is no reserved parking spot. Finally, we enter and disembark two hours late. That is nothing.

We haggle with autorickshaw drivers. They want fortunes to take us out to our friend's home. We finally choose a quiet, introspective youth lounging in his vehicle. He is pleased with our patronage and helps us—unaware of his impending clash with destiny. At the first major traffic light, he zooms through the red and straight into the arms of a very irate cop, soured by the chaos of Delhi traffic.

'Where is your license?' he demands.

A long explanation later, it transpires our driver does not possess one. And unceremoniously, he is hauled out and slapped. I intervene: no license is no license for brutality. The cop will not listen to me. He tells me this scoundrel is breaking the law. The driver clutches his leg, then mine, pleading and crying. Maureen tries to haul off the cop who is now brandishing his nightstick, beckoning another cop, and flagging down another auto. 'Sahib, sahib, save me, please.' I now have the boy touching my feet while I'm arguing for leniency. The cop has removed our cases to the other auto whose driver watches the scene placidly. 'They are going to confiscate my auto. How will I earn a living? I will be sent to prison.'

'Pay him,' Maureen says.

She means the driver but the cop won't have compassion. He shoves the money aside and escorts us to the waiting auto. The last we see of our driver he is being frogmarched between the two cops to—doubtless—jail. If that had been a fair measure of justice, I wouldn't feel this anger. If that youth had been the son of one of our politicians or industrialists or big shot Delhiwallahs, he would have been released with a polite reprimand. The cop knew he would have his back broken by a superior for having dared to discomfort a privileged boy. The poor have no such recourse to influence. Influence is the cash of Indian daily life. The bribe is, too, but it has its limitations. To know the right person—to have influence in oiling the cogs of India—is of far greater importance.

As we phut-phut through Delhi, our new driver, an older

man, reveals no compassion for the plight of his colleague. When we recount the incident to our friend he is equally abrupt: 'Serves him right. Those autorickshaw drivers are dangerous.'

Chetak

The next afternoon we return to Delhi station to await the Tamil Nadu Express from Madras. How can I not recognize my sister Nalini? She and Padmini are fixed more firmly into my consciousness than anyone else; apart from my father. They were the surrogates when my mother died and they comforted me. Both resemble her at different ages in her life: square-ish jaws, strong mouths, high cheekbones. Only in their eyes they sometimes seem to differ: Nalini's are more oriental, Padmini, occidental. Both have strong personalities, intimidating at times for a younger brother. And are fiercely protective of me. Nalini and I have up to now spent the most part of our lives separated not merely by distance but also by tradition. She grew up in my grandparents' home, out of bawling, stubborn choice as she and my mother it seems reached a mutual decision on this arrangement. (She must have been a precocious brat). From snatches of conversation, she did not get on with my mother and now not with my father. I have yet to understand why but deep down there is an animosity. Having lived with my grandparents, Nalini then married at sixteen (I was eight when this great event took place in our ancestral home. The event took days, hundreds came and hundreds were fed), the old ambition of Indian women and moved into her husband's home. So with this distance between us, though affection remained, we grew separate and apart.

She has always led the life of a princess. She moved from one great house to another and has never wanted for anything: sarees, jewellery, travel and later in life two sons. She and my other sister appear in one of my novels as forceful and strong characters but Nalini always overawes both Padmini and me. There is a harsh directness sometimes in her approach as if she has no time for the diplomatic manoeuvering of people and she is the only one who can tell me when I am a 'fool' without hedging the remark with politeness. But over the last few years I've noticed she has mellowed, grown more compassionate and in this re-discovery of her I've re-discovered a lot about India and about my own family traditions. She is, in the way of Indian women, the continuity with my past that broke when our mother died and her phenomenal memory can recount the minutest details of what occurred thirty or forty years ago. She is made in the mould of a Murari, quite adventurous, and full of curiosity for the strange and wonderful in India and the world. I suspect she would like to be as nomadic as me, but family and home bind her firmly to Madras. This is the first time really since childhood we have travelled together and I am looking forward to the journey with her. Maureen too, for thankfully they have much in common and have, over the years, become good friends.

We look down on the mass of people surging out of the Tamil Nadu express.It left Madras at dawn the day before, crawled up the face of India and arrived four hours late. We have spent the last hour, with countless others, darting from platform to platform as the New Delhi station announcer played checkers with the train: 'Arriving platform 1... arriving platform 6... arriving platform 14...' With each announcement the waiting south Indians surged from one platform to another. We are quite distinct here: smaller, darker, thinner, sarees differently tied, our tongue unlike any in the north. Maureen has found the waiting unsettling. She doesn't lack patience but has slowly grown angry at the bold stares of the passing males. Predatory, lusting, lascivious. No doubt they stare at Indian woman the same way. They have seen too many Playboy centrefolds and censored Hollywood movies.

Naturally Nalini does not spot this blonde European waiting for her. She has charged off the train and only by luck do we glimpse her, hurrying after the coolie in the opposite direction. She has seen another exit and is already out of the station. Who knows where she's going? Only we know the name of the hotel we have moved to from our friend's house. Tagging behind is her younger son, Lakshman. He is tall, quiet, shy and quite, quite spoilt. All Indian male children are spoilt, and they expand into spoilt adults. But I too was spoilt at his age: by sisters, grandmother, female cousins, doubly so because of my mother's death. It took years for me to escape the spoiling. Her son will be with us throughout this journey but because of his silences—he will only address his mother—I won't make further mention of him. You must assume his presence in the tale. We catch up with my sister before she disappears into the chaos of Delhi on her own strange journey.

Her embrace is restrained. Nalini cannot show affection openly. It remains behind barriers that are difficult to penetrate. She is open in her affection for her sons, and true love blossoms for her plump mongrel, which she stole from me when it was a pup. The hotel I've chosen is the Ashok Yatri Nivas, a brand new building on Ashoka road off Janpath, still in the throes of completion. The Indian government has built it for less affluent tourists. It is quite unprepared for the influx of young foreigners, crumpled, dishevelled, unwashed and a sprinkling of Indians in starched clothes. The staff is young, overworked and contemptuous of their patrons. On checking in, we must not only pay in advance but also leave a hefty deposit. The elevators are neurotic, but that can be forgiven. It is all still too new. The rooms are spare: a mattress on a raised platform, built-in cupboards, and a tiny bathroom. It is adequate, except there is no hot water. 'What do you expect?' The receptionist counters. 'You pay little and expect hot water all the time.' 'Is there any at all?' I admire my restraint. 'Between six and nine in the morning and seven and nine in the evening.' It sounds reasonable. However, it is eight in the evening and the water is cold. We bathe in the cold water, compromising with the implacable staff, but it only sets me up for my next confrontation with bureaucracy. After dinner, we stroll over to the Kanishka hotel—the wealthy companion to our cheap one. Both are government-owned but the contrast is between slabs of red stone and polished marble. The Kanishka's foyer is large as an airplane hangar, hung with chandeliers, carpeted, and decorated with all the beautiful artifacts India can produce. It is a five-star hotel, a favourite Indian term meaning par excellence although else where it would mean a decent Hilton. There is a pleasant bar in the mezzanine and over drinks we discuss our journey. They all accept our coming itinerary in blind faith. I am the elder male and leader of this expedition to Arjumand's grave.

When it's time to pay I offer an Indian Bank travellers' cheque. The waiter takes it but dolefully returns. 'We cannot accept it.' 'Why not? It's legal tender.' He shrugs and points to the cashier down in the foyer. The cashier repeats the waiter's words, and adds: 'We do not recognize Indian Bank.' 'Don't recognize it? But it's a government organization. Like yours.' 'I'm sorry. Talk to the manager.'

I should have by now recognized the beginning of a farce and the implacable nature of bureaucracy. The manager is a portly Sikh gentleman standing in the centre of the lobby under the chandelier. He has the courteous but steely manner that managers learn in Swiss hotel management classes. He watches my approach: trailed by two women, ire raised too. A minion is one step ahead of us, appraising him of the problem. The manager holds out his hand imperiously, like a magician about to make the irritation disappear, and studies the wad of cheques. Wishing only to please, I take out a letter of identification from my Indian Bank manager. This too is carefully scrutinized. I glance at my sister and Maureen as if to say the problem is solved. The Manager hands the cheques and the letter back to me reverently and announces: 'We find these cheques unacceptable.' 'But why?' 'How do we know you are the true owner?' 'I just gave you the letter.' 'Ahh, you only gave me the letter because the cheques are not genuine. If they were, you wouldn't have given me the letter.' None of us can think of a reply to such impeccable logic.

He looks delighted with the catch-22 he has presented to me, knowing full well that from here on the argument will spiral down into decreasing circles. 'So if I hadn't given you the identification letter, you would have accepted the cheques as payment?' 'I didn't say that.' He brooded. 'Maybe. No, I wouldn't have.' I pause. I glance at my sister who has lived all her life in India and is as mentally swift as Muhammad Ali's proverbial bee. She too has been momentarily silenced. 'Now… will you accept American Express travellers' cheques?' 'Certainly. Any denomination you wish.' He is already moving us towards the cashier. 'But I am the same person who just offered you those possibly forged Indian Bank travellers' cheques.' 'But these are American Express.' 'They can be forged, too.' He stops and for the first time makes a full appraisal of me. He notes that I have suddenly turned as implacable as his system. 'You're happy to take something foreign without a question,' Nalini says sharply. She intensely dislikes the Indian's love for things 'phoren'. 'But you won't accept something that is Indian.' 'That is because he showed me identification letter, Madam,' the manager returns to his battlement. 'There must be something wrong with those cheques.' He glances towards Maureen. 'We accept even Barclay Bank travellers' cheques. In sterling.' 'No you won't,' Maureen counters. 'You'll accept the Indian Bank cheques.' 'I won't. And you must pay your bill before you leave the premises.' 'I won't.' On such silly points of principle, I imagine, blood baths start. 'I offer perfectly legal tender and you refuse it. Why should I pay you with dollars or American Express?' 'Rupees then?' He cries as a last resort. 'Well ...' I linger in thought while he waits, wishing only to escape from this foyer and these persons upsetting him. 'I have these rupees in Indian Bank travellers' cheques only.' 'No.' 'Then no.' 'Where are you staying?' I detect a pleading tone. 'Next door.' I, too, compromise. 'If you send the bill to that hotel, I'll pay it in rupees. Cash.' 'Fine,' he barks and stalks off, leaving the minion to take down my room number. We exit the fine hotel, quite exhilarated by the skirmish and the victory.

The Chetak waits, besieged by hordes of people, and the familiar sounds and odours of an Indian railway station. Nalini goes up and pats the side of the carriage.

'Poor Chetak. Just look what they've done to you.'

Nalini knows most of the stirring tales of our heroes and heroines, though in this case Chetak is a war horse. It was the mount of Rana Pratap Singh of Udaipur. In a battle against the Mughal Emperor Aurangzeb, the prince was wounded and the horse, although dying of its own wounds, somehow helped the prince to remount and carried him away to safety. In memory of this brave animal the Indian Railways named a train after him.

As the train winds out of Delhi on its way to Chetak's spiritual home, Udaipur, I feel once more the loss of my mother. As a child, I too would have been told this tale, and countless others as well as our confusing mythology. In India, our umbilical thread to the past is through our mothers. While the female child learns the religious ceremonies and family traditions, the male child hears of its heroes. Fathers are too busy elsewhere to sit and tell these tales. And so I grew up with only a vague awareness about these acts of valour. Like my mother before, Nalini was told the stories of Rama and Sita, of how Lord Ganesh acquired that elephant's head, of what Lord Krishna, the charioteer, spoke of to Arjuna on the eve of battle, how to play the veena and sing in a sweet pure voice the bhajans of worship. She would have been taken to the Parthasarthy temple in Madras (where my family has always worshipped) and learnt the rituals of offerings and prayers. Nowadays, Nalini takes me there each time I visit Madras.

We have a compartment with four berths, quite spartan, with shoddy fixtures that have been painted a sickly sea green. When the ticket collector comes I ask him about our bedding. He punches our tickets, writes out another for our reservation, charging us extra, and says finally, 'You should have made that arrangement at the station, sir. There is no bedding on the train for you.'

It can't be helped. It's a long journey, stretching from this afternoon to the next morning. The landscape is desert: harsh and hostile, with Rajasthani women in brilliant swirls of colour—vibrant reds, yellows, blues, pinks—deliberately contrasting with the drab landscape. The vegetation is mostly cacti and 'flame of the forest', a tree that, seen at a distance in the jungle, creates the illusion of flames. The animal life consists mainly of camels and peacocks, rare creatures in south India. Dotted here and there, on bumps of earth like quotation marks, stand solitary fortresses. For centuries, they have guarded the barren earth that undulates below them, their long-deserted battlements facing north towards the routes of our conquerors. They look alike, these forts, high, granite, seemingly impregnable; and they fell like houses of cards to the Mughals. Infrequently through battle; mostly through intrigue. The Rajputs are our legendary warriors, the Hindu battlement against the Muslim conquerors, but they squandered their valour fighting between themselves. At times, through the haze of dust and heat, they appear occupied: villagers coming and going through the massive gates, children playing on the walls, but beneath the activity we sense the deathly silence of the past. We can only imagine the pageantry, the pennants, the soldiers, the glitter of armour.

'I wouldn't mind living in one of those,' I murmur. Nalini and Maureen raise their eyebrows at my grandiose pretentions. 'And what about taxes?' Nalini says, bitterly. She is very anti-tax as she shells out a fortune on her properties in Madras. 'Why do you think our princes are impoverished? They can't afford the taxes. God alone knows what grandmother would have done nowadays. She couldn't have lived in a stupid little apartment as we're expected to do today.' Nalini, as I mentioned, still retains princess tastes. But India has changed too swiftly even for her. The ground, literally, has been cut from beneath the feet of old land-owning families such as ours. We couldn't transform ourselves into industrialists or businessmen. We are the feudal past that is being, and should be, changed. We bicker briefly, amicably about taxes, our properties, my extravagance while Maureen, tiring of family tirades, retreats into her book. We had picked up *The Far Pavilions* in the Delhi station and after half an hour of reading, I hurled it across the compartment. Maureen too, more knowledgeable now of India, hurls it away a couple of times but with little else to read reluctantly picks it up. English fiction about India reveals a truly abysmal ignorance of the country, the people, the customs, everything. When the Englishman first came to India in the 16th and 17th centuries, there was a true integration of the cultures. Apart from inter-marriage, the Englishman learnt and wrote Urdu poetry (or whatever language they were surrounded by), studied our customs, understood the philosophy of our religion and art. The Ashokan edicts were first translated from Maghadi Prakrit by James Prinsep. And then, dread! The tea clippers made the journey between England and India comfortable and swift, and the English woman, the memsahib, turned up on our shores and, like Eve entering Eden, hurled ... the Indian? The Englishman? out of this paradise. This pale and prim creature, yoked to Victorian prudery, could not compare herself to the exotic Indian woman or grasp the complexities of Indian life. She, instead, preferred to withdraw into an enclave she formed for herself, drawing the Englishman in with her. India conquers by absorption and because the English refused to be absorbed they were rejected. Once, when my father and I were discussing the English in India, I asked him how he would define their attitude. 'They came to India to recreate the aristocracy they could never ever belong to in England,' he told me. I remember being struck into silence by the perception of this old man's observation.

When the train stops at Alwar, with a palace/fortress overlooking the railway station, I hop off. Maureen feels peckish and I buy some hot samosas but neither Nalini nor I eat them while Maureen only takes a nibble of one. As we creep west, dusk falls and it turns quite chilly. I regret not having booked the bedding in the railway station, but warm myself with a couple of whiskeys from my pint bottle. And as I watch the shadows lengthen and gradually blend into night, with the sun fiery for a moment or two and then suddenly sliding out of sight, I think again of Arjumand.

She waited five years for her prince. Like this desert, barren, alone. In those times, a girl was married by twelve or fourteen, and had borne children by sixteen. She had to be sustained by love and the hope that the prince still remembered her from that night of the Royal Meena bazaar. He himself was preoccupied with reaching for the throne. Khusrau, Shah Jahan's elder brother, believed that his grandfather Akbar had chosen him as the rightful heir to the Mughal throne, and not Jahangir. He had rebelled against Jahangir and, when an attempted assassination of his father failed, Jahangir had him blinded and chained to a soldier as his punishment for the attempt. Obeying the Timurid law, he did not kill Khusrau. Because of that Jahangir had chosen Shah Jahan as his favourite son—above three other brothers—and he had given the crown prince the jagir of Hissan Feroz. He was also governor of Lahore and, as I mentioned before, married to a Persian princess. Arjumand remained hidden both from society and us behind the walls of the zenana. Her close friends were married off (arranged, naturally) while she was already turning into a spinster, filled with doubts about her stubbornness, also continuously reminded and nagged by her mother that she was ageing into an ancient crone whom no one would ever want to marry. Even Mehrunissa had by now married Jahangir.

Poor Arjumand. The wheels of the train, in that hypnotic way they have of reading one's innermost thoughts, repeat: 'poor Arjumand ... poor Arjumand'.

With night comes dinner, and a menu unchanged from the Grand Trunk; chicken curry, rice, chapatis, spinach; all for four rupees. After dinner we lock and bolt our doors and windows. India hasn't changed much since Arjumand's days. Dacoits still roam the country, and if in those days they attacked the travellers of caravans, they now choose trains. The newspapers often carry lurid stories of dacoits holding up passengers and robbing the women of their thalis and nose rings and earrings, and men of their cash. I expect to sleep well for I am now in the familiar womb with my ears filled with the soft and soothing sounds of my childhood. But it has turned bitterly cold and we huddle under coats and pullovers, dozing as best we can and woken often by the bustle of stations that never need sleep.

We wake at dawn as the train slides into Chittorgarh. Just north of the railway station, dominating the town and the horizon is the massive ruined fort/palace of Chittorgarh. It was built on top a rock hill 500 feet high with cliff-like sides. The winding walls of the fort, covering three and a half miles of the summit have been embedded into the rock and appear to be a natural part of the hill. The chilly early morning mist hangs over the battlements and turrets, like a mourning veil, partially obscuring the broken walls and its jungle flanks from the prying eye of my camera. It dozes in the long past. Every Indian child has been nurtured on the stories of this ruined silence. Thrice her defenders have preferred death to surrender. It was up there, behind those high walls, that in 1303 the beautiful princess Padmini chose to commit jauhar rather than be ravished by the Pathan conqueror Ala-ud-din Khilji. The tale goes thus: He could not conquer Chittorgarh but, having heard of Padmini's great beauty, begged the Udaipur prince for permission to gaze upon her. Only then would he withdraw from the siege. The prince gave permission and through this deception Khilji managed to enter the fort. But no Muslim could ever look upon a Rajput princess, so Padmini permitted him to gaze on her reflection in a mirror. He became so besotted that he continued the siege and finally breached the walls, but before he could claim Padmini she and other Rajput women commited jauhar in an underground cave. In 1535, Bahadur Shah, Sultan of Gujarat, also laid siege to the fort. The then Queen-Mother, Jawahir Bai, led a charge and was slain. Once more as the fort began to fall, the Rajput women committed jauhar. (13,000 this time). And in that battle 32,000 Rajputs died. Finally, in 1567, the Mughal emperor Akbar laid a year-long siege. The Sisodia escaped to build another fort in Udaipur, and those left behind defended the fort to the last man and woman. Akbar then, quite out of character, sacked the fort.

As the train slides away, the sun has burnt off the mist. The fort's walls are dark and mossed, monkeys are silhouetted on the battlements and it seems as if the noise of battle still echoes on and on.

Udaipur

Soon we arrive in Udaipur, where Nalini pats Chetak a fond goodbye. It is because of Arjumand that I am here. We decide not to stay in the Lake Palace Hotel. This island of marble luxury on the Pichola Lake seems an unnecessary extravagance. Instead we chose the Lakshmi Vilas Palace Hotel, a former royal hunting lodge. We get there by our staple transport, the autorickshaw, and find it's less a palace and more a generously sized bungalow perched on a hill, overlooking the lake and the town. Past the foyer and in the reception we flinch at the sight of two large tiger skins decorating the walls. There are a couple of ancient muskets too, reminding us of the sport of our princes.

The sleepless cold night has been debilitating and apart from that Maureen has also caught a bug—remember the samosa I bought in Alwar and which she nibbled, travelling is fraught with such tiny traps—and is running a temperature. Nalini, the practical wife of a doctor, immediately unearths tablets of various sorts. But Maureen refuses to remain in bed and insists on accompanying us to the Maharaja's palace.

The old city, founded by the Prince Udai Singh who escaped Chittorgarh and Akbar's wrath, is encircled by the fortress walls. The city has long since grown and now spills out and over these ancient barriers. The interior is small and crowded, with narrow winding streets. The tourist must be a familiar sight here for every second hole-in-the-wall is an antique shop plastered with blue American Express stickers. But I haven't come to merely sight-see. Arjumand came here twice. The first time, around 1614, she accompanied Shah Jahan and the Mughal army on their battle against the Mewar Rajputs.

Arjumand's patience was finally rewarded. Shah Jahan returned his Persian princess to Persia, and married the girl he had fallen in love with. The event took place in 1612 and the pomp and ceremony was beyond our imaginings. Gifts of gold howdahs and saddles and chairs, magnificent jewellery, slaves, elephants and horses were presented to the couple. Thousands upon thousands were fed, and lakhs of rupees distributed to the poor. Arjumand must have been ecstatically happy that day. At the ripe age of seventeen, she had become the wife of the crown prince of India. On the day of the marriage, her name changed from Arjumand to Mumtaz Mahal, the Jewel of the Palace. During her life, poets wrote about her beauty, her grace, her compassion and her deep love for her husband. And then came the miscarriages and child births. Her first child to survive, Jahanara, was born in 1614. In 1615, she had a son, Dara, their favourite. Twelve others followed; in all seven children survived, seven died.

The Mewar Rajputs were a constant thorn in the side of the Mughal emperors. Shah Jahan's first assignment after marrying Arjumand was the then impossible task of subduing these troublesome enemies. This was Mehrunissa's plan, in the hope that Shah Jahan would fail. Of course, the moment he and his huge Mughal army came into view, the Mewar Sisodia withdrew into this fortress town of Udaipur. Shah Jahan laid siege but it was a hopeless stalemate as the town was well-stocked with food and water and threatened to hold out forever. This exercise was to be a test of Shah Jahan's skill. Arjumand could have remained contentedly and comfortably back in the Agra palace but she was a woman, as we have seen, of some strength of character. She accompanied Shah Jahan to this battle front and waited patiently by his side until he thought up a new strategy. Possibly, she might have given him the idea. The siege was failing so Shah Jahan, imitating the methods of his ancestor Timur-i-Leng, began to lay waste the surrounding countryside. He burnt crops, killed cattle, destroyed villages. The brave Rajput men were all here in Udaipur and could only watch helplessly until the Sisodia capitulated in order to save his land and people.

Shah Jahan was wise enough to understand the need for conciliation now. Like Akbar before him, Jahangir, who took credit for the victory, treated his enemy generously. Mewar could keep all their territories and pay a nominal sum of money as tribute to the Mughal king and hand over the crown prince, Karan Singh, to stay as a 'guest' of the Emperor. Thus began a long friendship between Shah Jahan and Karan Singh and when the time came for Shah Jahan to seek shelter from his father's wrath, he and Arjumand came here for refuge.

I had stopped off in Udaipur not only to get a sense of the place Arjumand had visited but because I wanted to meet the Maharaja. It's not an impossible matter to meet an Indian prince; it just depends on his mood. They are, for the most part, insufferably arrogant, undependable, and acutely conscious of their rusty titles. One must have a desperate need for this royalty in order to tolerate them. My need was historical. He is a descendant of Karan Singh and could have a historical memory of Arjumand and Shah Jahan. I also needed his permission to get to the Lake Palace. Not the hotel, the Jag Niwas Palace, now crowded with French tourists, but the one beyond: Jag Mandir. Apart from sheltering the prince and Arjumand, it was also the refuge of English memsahibs during the Mutiny of 1857. The old city palace, in which our prince resides, is the haunt of tourists, but beyond a gate, past some beautiful Guernsey cross-breed cows, is the Maharaja's new palace. The entrance is guarded by a chowkidar dressed in khaki, a most unmilitary-looking man. He tells us to make enquiries at a small building, standing apart from the main palace. On the verandah, comfortable in cane chairs, are two elderly gentlemen watching my approach. They are both plump and white haired, with the benign faces of retirees. Both too wear blinding white slacks and bush shirts. I cannot help but think of them as Tweedledum and Tweedledee.

'I would like to meet His Highness, talk to him and also obtain permission to visit Jag Mandir.' I am contemplated sleepily. Tweedledum, to the right, replies, 'It is under repair. And His Highness is out-of-station.' 'When will he return?' They shrug. Tweedledee answers finally, 'You must enquire of his ADC.' 'And to visit Jag Mandir?' 'That too.' I am pointed down the road. The ADC is somewhere beyond. I wander down the curving road and past the palace, brooding and silent. Not a sign of life to be seen anywhere in the countless windows or balconies that overlook the lake. Pigeons strut on the rooftop and the window sills. It all looks a pretty facade. The road leads me into a deserted back yard. There are rows of rooms, with locked doors, and in the shade of a peepul tree stands a small cottage. Its outer wall is lapped gently by the lake water and a rowing boat rises and falls, beckoning me to abandon formality and row myself over. Instead I ring the bell. No one emerges. Finally, I give up but as I wander back, a postman strolls past.

'You will find the ADC in his office. Come.' We go back, past the sitting gentlemen who still gaze at me incuriously. The postman leads me to a side entrance of the palace and down a gloomy corridor into an office filled with files and files and a lone youth contemplating them sadly. He looks like someone who should be playing truant or possibly he dreams of what it would be like to be the prince, rather than a clerk. The sun touches his desk, but he remains in the shadow and only slowly gives me his attention. 'His Highness's ADC is out-of-station,' he informs me. 'When does he return?' He shrugs. This, I feel, would certainly defeat any enquiring army looking for someone of authority. I return to the elderly gentlemen. 'The ADC is out-of-station,' I accuse them impatiently. 'We know.' 'Then can I find a Mr Dayala?' I consult my notebook. I had been given his name as an authority on Udaipur. 'I am Mr Dayala,' Tweedledum reluctantly admits. It is obviously his time in the sun, a quiet period of life for contemplation. 'Then you can help me…' I reel off my requirements: How did Arjumand live while she was here? Who looked after her?

How many children did Arjumand have with her at the time? Are there any portraits of her here? Any other evidence, written diaries, about her? What did they do when they were here? When Shah Jahan defeated Mewar did ...

'The Mughals,' Mr Dayala interrupts me fiercely, 'never defeated Mewar. We did not cooperate with them, like those Jaipur princes. They gave the Muslims their women in marriage.' He has spoken with derision as if the incident had but recently occurred and not four centuries ago. The contempt for the Jaipur clan of princes is barely concealed. 'I am not an authority on such matters, sir,' he says in a more casual tone. 'You should consult Dr Jhawali. He is our local historian.' 'Or Mr Chakravarthi, the museum curator,' Tweedledee adds helpfully. They tell me where to find both men.

Maureen, Nalini and Lakshman have been waiting patiently in the car. I confess my failure morosely. I no longer seem to have the patience for these matters. Possibly I have lived away too long. If I had remained in India such circuitous dialogues would have become a customary part of my daily life, and I would have accepted it all fatalistically. Nalini waves away the irritation. She is eager to explore the old palace, and while the three of them set off down the ancient corridors, I continue my search, this time for Mr Chakravarthi. I'm sure he will be more amenable. The curator's office is a large sunny room, overlooking the lake. A youngish man sits behind a large desk, looking more authoritative than the last one. His clothes look frozen in starch. His in-tray is empty, his out-tray filled. 'Mr Chakravarthi?' 'Mr Chakravarthi is no longer the curator here. I am. I believe he has been transferred to Jodhpur.' So much for my two authoritative figures who I feel, bitterly, were aware of this fact. I settle down. A curator is a curator. Now, my questions. He listens patiently, continually polite and smiling. When I halt, suddenly uncertain with this silence, his smile turns apologetic. 'I know nothing about Udaipur's history. I am new here.'

Fatalistic now, I rise and leave. The apologetic smile remains fixed on his face. From the emptiness of his desk, I suspect he will fill his tenure here, a nice government job, always ignorant of Udaipur history. The museum and the palace console me. Apart from the paintings of past princes and a massive array of ancient weapons, I find, sitting in a glass case in a corner, the actual turban of Shah Jahan. It is faded and dusty, an indeterminate colour, woven with gold thread. It's flat, deflated, forlorn. I think: Arjumand saw this turban placed on her husband's head, possibly touched it herself. I voice my complaint.'It doesn't look like an emperor's turban.' 'Well, what do you expect after 400 years?' Nalini comments. I'm not sure. We always expect magnificence from emperors, not a sad bundle of cloth resembling a stuffed serpent. Shah Jahan and Karan Singh had exchanged turbans as a token of their friendship. So this one sat on Karan Singh's head, briefly, and his descendants prized this gift enough to ensure it would survive all these centuries.

The palace is still beautiful. The murals, painted hundreds of years ago, are still vibrant, still fresh. The Manak Mahal is filled with figures of glass, and the Moti Mahal is decorated with a thousand mirrors. Architecturally the palace is a very clever maze. It was built encircling a hill, although while in it, you never get that impression. It is only when you reach the top that you discover the gardened crest of the hill filled with trees and flowering shrubs, surrounded by a square of marble pavilions and delicate archways. There is a marble fountain to rest by, and a view of the whole city, and beyond to the hazy surrounding hills.

We take the launch out to the Lake Palace Hotel for lunch. It is so easy to imagine those princes strolling through all this magnificence and their lovely women lounging in their marble rooms, and the courtyards filled with gardens and fountains. The latest James Bond movie has just recently been shot here and the waiter is only too delighted to tell us all about it. The crew spent many months filming in and around the palace. (Months later we see the film, *Octopussy*. It could just as well have been shot in Pinewood Studios or a Hollywood back lot. In fact, so confident are the filmmakers in their ignorance of India that they do not even bother with continuity: Agra becomes Varanasi, Udaipur Jaipur, this palace another and of course, Pinewood). The food in this exquisite hotel is quite indifferent, with the chicken mughlai quite suspect. Tourists arrive, occupy a large table and pull out cavernous cases, bottles of Perrier or Vichy water. I presume even James Bond didn't risk drinking the local water.

We return to our hotel. From our window, we can look down on a different shore of Lake Pinchola. There is another island: a landscaped garden with a temple at one end. Totally deserted. On the crest of a distant hill is the black prancing silhouette of Chetak.

Having defeated Mewar…well, depending on who is evaluating that event but to be fair I too will compromise and call it an 'arrangement' with Mewar…Shah Jahan and Arjumand, accompanied by the young Karan Singh, travelled from here to Ajmer. There they were feted by the Emperor Jahangir and his Empress Nur Jahan. Arjumand would have been pregnant again. For the first eight years of their marriage this was her permanent condition. It was their lust for each other, not merely romantic love, that was eventually to tragically destroy her.

The second time they came to Udaipur, around 1623, fate dealt them a joker.

They were living in Burhanpur when Jahangir (probably Mehrunissa) ordered Shah Jahan to send his army to Kandahar to be commanded by Jahangir. Shah Jahan refused and earned the wrath of the Emperor Jahangir, who now called his once-favourite son 'bi-daulat' (the wretch). Having been refused the command of the Mughal force against the Persian army, Shah Jahan had thoughts of seizing the treasury in Agra. Jahangir sent a force, commanded by Shah Jahan's tutor and friend Mahabat Khan, to bring Shah Jahan to heel. They fought and Shah Jahan lost against the superior strength of the Mughal army. He escaped capture and fled from Burhanpur with Mahabat Khan in pursuit. Shah Jahan's biographer Inayat Khan, in the *Shah Jahan Nama,* tells that Shah Jahan wept and kissed his faithful and loyal elephant, Bairam, a sad farewell. Bairam, in turn, cried too, and wrapped its truck lovingly around Shah Jahan.

Arjumand was doubtless a woman with a zest for adventure. She could have remained behind in Burhanpur with her children, instead she went on the run with him too. There is no doubt she would have been unharmed. The Mughals scrupulously obeyed the Timurid law—harm not your own blood. They might have pursued rebellious sons, blinded them even, but never, until Shah Jahan killed his brother Khusrau bringing disaster down on himself and his children, did they murder each other. Jahangir would not have touched a hair of Arjumand's or her children's heads. She, Shah Jahan and the children spent many years, travelling over those dirt roads and through jungles, smothered by the Indian dust. Arjumand would have travelled in a carriage pulled by either an elephant, a camel or bullocks with a minimum of slaves and attendants: a maid or two, possibly an eunuch, and her personal hakim. They were always one jump ahead of the pursuing Mahabat Khan. Finally they reached Udaipur, were welcomed by Karan Singh, and rested in his lake palace, a marble cloud afloat on water. Even if they had travelled directly from Burhanpur, and not zig-zagged over central India, it would have taken them three months to cover the 570 kilometres. The luxury and comfort of the Udaipur palace must have been an enormous respite from being shaken constantly by her carriage. She lay still then for a few months on silken divans, soothed by marble and the quiet slaps of water, entertained by Rajasthani folk singers and dancers. For four years, from 1622 to 1626, the family was chased from one end of central India to the other by the Mughal army under the command of General Mahabat Khan. Children still tumbled from Arjumand's fertile womb but they all died except for a son, Murad, in 1624. In 1626, Shah Jahan sent a message to his father begging forgiveness. Jahangir grumbled in his biography: 'In ailing health I have to ride into battle aginst my son.' But, equably now, through Mehrunissa's advice, he accepted the offer of peace. Mehrunissa saw her power being frittered away in this endless pursuit of Shah Jahan, and the rise in power of Mahabat Khan. Through Jahangir she issued a firman stipulating the terms for peace: Shah Jahan was to send two of his sons, Dara and Aurangzeb to court, and he should take up the governorship of Balaghat, a most miserable jagir. Shah Jahan kissed the firman to show his agreement and sent his sons, but managed to stall his move to Balaghat for a year, until Jahangir died in his favourite place, Kashmir.

Years later, when Shah Jahan was the emperor, he visited Udaipur again. According to the 17th-century Italian adventurer Niccolao Manucci in his *Storia do Mogor,* when the Emperor travelled—even on a hunt—his entourage of soldiers, servants, elephants, camels burdened with gold and silver and state papers, women, slaves and musicians took half a day to pass a fixed point. At the head rode the Emperor, preceded by nine elephants, each bearing the Mughal Standard of the crouching lion set against a rising sun; then four more carried green flags depicting the sun. Next came nine riderless white stallions bearing gold saddles, stirrups and bits, and behind them rode two horsemen. One carried a banner bearing Shah Jahan's title 'King of the World', the other rode with the dundhubi which he struck regularly to warn of the approach of the Great Mughal. Thirty men ran ahead on foot, scattering scented water.

I leave Maureen restlessly dozing, perspiring from her bug. Down the hotel corridor, past the shops filled with curios, which also have some authentic antique bits and pieces, Nalini is browsing and arguing with the youth who runs the shop. 'Suppose,' she is enquiring, 'a foreigner wants to buy that.' She points to an old brass chain from which hangs an appropriately ancient oil lamp. 'He cannot, Madam.' I feel as if they have been circling for some time. She is always worried that the foreigners, because of their money, steal away bits and pieces of her India. I agree with her. Temples and museums are robbed daily, and those gods and goddesses carved by artists a thousand years ago, reappear in New York or London or Paris. The government did pass a law prohibiting the export of antiques, but greed overwhelms such pieces of paper. The greed of temple priests, the greed of museum officials, the greed of customs officials. 'Why not? He pays you the money and puts it in his case and is back abroad.' He pulls out a sheaf of faded forms. 'These are the papers for that. I am regularly checked by government officers, Madam. If the piece is missing I must account for it.' Of course, the ordinary tourist poses little threat. All he wants is a piece of silk, a bit of silver, a brass lamp, a souvenir as proof he was once in India. It is the professional that she is worrying about. Nalini is an avid collector. In her home she has a huge collection of brass artefacts, paintings, sculpture, furniture. She loves Indian things with a passion. She pours her energy into haunting the bazaars and lanes and tiny khadais for those bits and pieces, inexpensive, and ignored or overlooked by the antique dealers who always seem to be either a step behind her or ahead. Though wealthy, she remains a careful acquisitor, not willing to spend thousands. Beauty, and a bargain, are her criteria. We have spent many hours together browsing the bazaars of Madras. There are no bargains in the hotel shops, only tourist prices.

The afternoon slips by on cups of tea, sitting on the threadbare lawn in the shade, looking down at the swimming pool. Three Europeans, a man and two women, lie beside it blistering to a tandoori red. Neither Nalini nor can I bear to watch this self-immolation for long and impatient with escaping time, we drive out to an archaeological site at the city limit. In front of it is a small bungalow, which houses the finds from the dig. In the cool empty rooms we drift by dusty glass cases containing clay urns and shards of pottery and arms and legs of gods. These are all that remain of the ancient settlement of Ahar.

A hundred yards away, abandoned to goats, are the chhattris of the ruling Maharanas. They vary in size, though not in shape. There could be fifty or even a hundred of these square-based, steep-stepped, high-domed structures. We enter through a break in the wall, and follow well-trodden paths meandering through these minor ruins. Some, the better preserved, are made of marble; others, fallen and sprouting vines, of brick and chunam. In the evening light, there is a ghostly, forgotten feel. We climb the steps to a newish one, built for the present prince's father. It is the highest and from there we view the jumble of ruins: no patterns, no symmetry: where there was space, they were built. The centre of the floor of this one is ringed by pigeon shit. A perfect circle, only one or two spatters out of alignment. Above our heads, sitting in cooing tranquility on a ledge that runs around the dome, are the culprits—

eyeing us with that cocked look of vanity. We spend an hour, aimlessly climbing up and climbing down; there's nothing to read, nothing to really see, although here and there are the signs of worship. Saffron, kum-kum, a shattered coconut. It's the silence, the visual continuity of one princely line over five hundred years long that holds our attention. I suppose it was here, standing in this haunted memory of princes, that we both felt a sense of deep belonging to India.

This is a different India to the one we come from, yet the bond here is that our history is intertwined. If one is to define India and Indians in any way, for we are impossibly diverse, it is this commonality of history. It is our knowledge of their deeds and their knowledge of ours, schoolchildren learning by rote their history lessons, this is the thread between us all. In this awareness of history as we tread along ancient pathways, we're both rediscovering our India. We could have come here at another time, gazed upon this jumble of memories, and only hazily identified with the specific. But here is also the memory of Karan Singh. Which is his chhattri? I don't know but I'm comforted that he is preserved here somehow though his ashes have long slipped down the waters and into the seas. 'I'm so glad I came with you,' Nalini says. 'We read about all these people and never come to see where they lived and died. We Indians prefer to dash off to New York or Europe.' She snorts, 'As if their history is richer than ours.' Having quite rightly put the world in its place, we wind through the narrow pathway and back out onto the road. It feels as if we have moved centuries in a few steps.

The next morning, early, I visit the railway station to

reserve our sleepers for the journey to Ajmer. Arjumand had been there with Shah Jahan. The clerk behind the counter meticulously takes down my booking for bedding. 'It will be done, sir,' he says with calm politeness. Assured of a comfortable journey, I return to haunt and harry the palace officials but no one will allow me to visit the lake palace. So near, yet unreachable. I sit on a wall, and watch the palace, hoping it will escape its moorings and drift to within reach. Nothing moves on it; the distant gardens and marble alcoves and chambers remain deserted.

The bazaar nearby is irresistible to Nalini and Maureen (pale still, slightly feverish, determined). What is there to find? Numerous paintings on cloth, costing hundreds of rupees, while if you step outside the town's limits or even remain in Delhi, you can buy them from the Rajasthani village women for a tenth of the price. The houses here are built on the slope of a hill, and are a maze of corridors, rooms, courtyards that rise imperceptibly, in imitation of the Maharana's palace. (It would be the reverse. The princes learned from their people, not the people from their princes). Women and children watch us exploring, peering into darkened rooms, and exclaiming over old carvings that are part of the buildings and were placed there as mere decoration. Now of course, they are works of art, often chipped out and sold in the antique shops. Nalini would be more than happy to tear down a building or two to get her hands on an intricately carved balcony or an elaborate window frame, both now, though neglected, still revealing their beauty. In a small back room, a man draped in the false joviality of a salesman and his assistant—a boy of ten or so with a round, cheery face—open a chest and hurl out bolts of paintings on cloth: silk and cotton; wall sizes, hankerchief sizes; emperors, ladies of court, prancing Chetak, gold-draped elephants and Rajput princes cascade at our feet. The small gloomy room turns awash with bright, rich colours. 'Who paints them?' I ask, for though some are crudely executed others are finely painted, immensely detailed, exquisite. 'Local people, sahib,' the merchant waves vaguely around. He is in his twenties, and fluent not only in English, but I suspect in other tourist tongues as well. He pats the boy beside him. 'He too is an artist and paints these.' The boy beams, 'I am learning from my teacher.' He expounds further, 'I work on many paintings with other boys like me. We learn.' As in the old ateliers, the boy will imitate the work of his teacher. The older artist will draw the general outlines, maybe even the details, and the colouring will be done by one of the boys. Art, here in the kingdom of Mewar, was patronized by the ruler. However, due to the continual hostilities between this kingdom and the expanding Mughal (and Muslim) empire, there was little artistic cross-fertilization between these Rajput painters and those who worked in the Mughal ateliers. Mughal art is mainly to be found in the miniatures of court scenes, elephant fights, hunts. The Rajput artists here—unlike their counterparts in Jaipur who, due to the close contact of their rulers with the Mughal emperors, quickly learnt the new techniques—had to wait a century before that influence entered their paintings. The scenes they would depict were religious for the most part and though talented, somewhat careless in their work. It was only in the 18th century, with the Mughal Empire in decline, that those influences came to Mewar and we see their court scenes and other miniatures. Until then cloth painting, especially depicting Krishna in a pastoral setting, was their speciality. The cheerful boy, helping to sell these cloths for one thousand, two thousand rupees—'Yes, American Express accepted'—is merely a link in the continuity of Rajput painters.

While Nalini bargains, I wander up a flight of stairs, expecting to enter a room but instead finding a courtyard. The layers of rooms and courtyards seem quite magical, a puzzle of buildings I cannot decipher. A beautiful woman, wearing those vivid splashes of colour, bathes her contented baby: pouring water from a brass lota onto it. The courtyard is otherwise deserted, and standing in the shadow of the doorway, I feel like an intruder. What I see is tranquil, comforting and echoing continuity. The tableau is permanent; only the figurines change. Aware of the watcher, the woman glances up, smiles shyly, and with a pang of regret for having disturbed the innocent scene, I watch her melt back into the shadows of the room behind. When I return to the commercial transaction below, my sister has bought two paintings: one the size of a hankerchief, another a portrait. 'I don't know why. I already have half a dozen at home.' But she feels that having come to Rajasthan, she should buy them.

From Udaipur of course, there are hundreds of other places to visit. 'Go to Jaisalmer... go to Rajnagar... go to Eklinji lake... go to...' But we cannot go to all these places, the journey is set, the destination Ajmer. In India, one must always know exactly where one is going, for otherwise it is a country in which one can wander and wonder forever for there is so much to see. History here lies like silt, endless layers, endless ruins, palaces, forts, temples, pavilions, natural wonders. It is as if they tumbled out of a shaker and lie all over in abundance.

Ajmer

Once more we vault onto Chetak, now returning from his run to Allahabad. Having stored our luggage I anxiously search for the train attendant and find him lounging near a chai cart. 'You did get our order for bedding?' 'What bedding? You must talk to the stationmaster.' I find the stationmaster in his office, and he smiles sweetly, shaking his head even before I have completed my enquiry. 'No bedding order has been received by this office.' 'But I gave it yesterday to the booking clerk.' 'Ahh, you should not have given it to him. You should have given it to this office. And,' he adds courteously, 'it must be done in writing two weeks before departing time of train.'

I retreat, defeated, fuming. Knowledge is so valuable here that it is handed out in tiny morsels. Why did the booking clerk, knowing full well the regulations, take my request and enter it in his book? I presumed doubtless he was just fulfilling my wish, aware that nothing would happen. The train attendant, meanwhile, unsettled by my enquiry, has summoned the ticket collector. 'You shouted at him,' the ticket collector accuses me. He is in his thirties, with a bristling moustache, a mouth lusciously red with paan, features contorted in high indignation, clutching bundles of papers tightly. Behind, glaring at me, is the attendant. 'I didn't shout at him. I just asked for our bedding.' 'That is not his job. If he has the order papers he will provide bedding. Now it is too late. In future you will not shout at the attendant.' 'Listen,' I am now shouting, as are Maureen and Nalini who have joined battle, 'I didn't shout at that little bastard. I made a request and he referred me to the stationmaster. How dare you come here and accuse me of shouting at him?' Under assault now from all three, he retreats muttering away under his breath. The train attendant has, very wisely, disappeared as we all want to wring his neck. As Chetak is due to arrive in Ajmer at 2.30 in the morning, we doze in snatches, huddled in our coats. I vow that next time I will get bedding, even if it kills me.

At Ajmer, we stumble off the train and into autorickshaws. There is only one hotel in town—the Rajasthan State guest house, a sprawling building set in a large garden. It was here in Ajmer that Arjumand watched the impressive ceremony of Emperor Jahangir confirming that the Prince Khurram was his heir to the Mughal Empire. Jahangir was of course delighted with 'his' victory over the Mewar Rajputs. He came to Ajmer to accept the gifts and offer hospitality to Karan Singh who was described as a 'wild looking youth'. This durbar was held in Akbar's palace. It is the first place we visit in the morning only to find it is a small square fort made of sandstone with an intricately carved gateway. Within is a small, square building, made partially of marble with that familiar detail of archways and finely carved screens. The fort is now a museum with the exhibits of weapons and pottery arranged in the old barrack rooms that run alongside the walls, while the central building is the office of the archaeological department.

Here, in front of his nobles, and Arjumand and her aunt Nur Jahan, Jahangir greeted his successful son. Shah Jahan was permitted to be seated in front of his father, within the gold railing and below the throne set in the high alcove. Jahangir gave a long speech in which, with the usual modesty of emperors, he proclaimed the victory as his own—even boasting that he had succeeded where his father, Akbar, had failed.

He then descended from the alcove and, accompanied by slaves carrying trays of precious stones, gold and silver coins, approached Shah Jahan. He embraced his son and then, scooping up diamonds and emeralds and rubies and pearls, poured them over Shah Jahan's turbaned head. He repeated the gesture with the gold and silver coins, and then gave Shah Jahan permission to pitch the red tent. Scarlet was the emperor's colour; red for the crown prince of the Mughal Empire. He also raised his son to the position of commander of 10,000 zat (one zat equalled 1000 horsemen and the equivalent pay to support them). Arjumand would have been seated with the other women behind the marble screen, proudly watching the elevation of her husband. At the time, she wouldn't have known how fickle an emperor's love could be.

Ajmer, a pretty name, is a small town, and though seemingly remote and ignored by most tourists for it lacks the essential ingredients for them—romantic palaces and air-conditioned hotels—it never lacked attention from invading forces. For eight centuries countless armies have marched and counter-marched, conquered and lost and re-conquered this strategically located town. It was a springboard for the Mughal military adventures into Rajasthan, especially against Udaipur, and further west into Gujarat. The British too maintained a military base here and back for lunch at our guest house we are not surprised to be served by an 'English' boy. He has blonde hair, pale blue eyes and his cheeks are as flushed as an English rose. He could be our 20th-century Kim though he would stand out a mile in any bazaar. None of the staff appears to note his difference and his command of English is almost non-existent.

I once went to school with boys like him. In my childhood, a brief four years after Independence, schools like mine were enclaves of England, little islands in the vastness of India on which the British still had a toehold. We attended chapel, wore house colours and lustily sang our school and house songs. It seemed to me then that an 'English' education was meant to be a fervent experience for a boy, binding him emotionally to the old school tie. The English boys were all awaiting their passages to England. Impatient to go 'home' to a land few, if any, had ever seen. Most were in their final year of school and as a very small boy, I never got close enough to authenticate their lineage. However, much closer, at the next desk or in the row behind, were the Anglo-Indian boys. (The word had two meanings, depending on whether it was used in England or India. In England it meant those who were pure English serving out in India, and in India it meant a different kind of people, half-castes). There is a history to be written about the Anglo-Indians, trapped between two opposing forces, neither one nor the other and shunned by both, stranded in the twilight of the British empire and yearning to go 'home' too. The British deliberately used them as a buffer between themselves and the Indians. The Anglo-Indians served in sensitive posts, though lower down in the ranks than the Englishmen—the police and the railways. They lived in enclaves of their own, identifying not with the land of their birth but with the alien forces who, as caste-conscious as any Brahmin, held them at bay and even treated them with cruel contempt. They were a constant reminder to the memsahibs, who ruled the English social life in India with rods of iron etiquette, that their men once consorted with Indian women.

These boys in my class constantly spoke of relatives in 'the UK', their plans to leave and, as they were not particularly well off, the scramble for their passage money to England. Of course none of us Indians could understand this terrible yearning in them. We were newly-minted patriots, Nehru's speeches reverberating in our souls, Gandhi still fresh in our memories. We mixed in school and on the playing fields and seldom invited them into our homes. Their rooms were small, humble ones decorated in English nostalgia: prints of England, photographs of them with Englishmen as reverently framed as if all the English were royalty, and photographs of their luckier relatives who had gone 'home' and sent back fragment pictures of themselves in Trafalgar Square or Piccadilly. I still remember their names too—Laird, a thin, almost tubercular boy, Nyss, a thickset and clever son of a priest, the Lovegrove and Ferdinand brothers (these two a veritable tribe which stretched from senior year down to my level and whose homes were in Hyderabad).

Then one day we would walk into class and notice the empty desk and hear that the boy had gone home for ever. The boy serving us lunch will never go home. He is home. Indian in every mannerism though doubtless, when he glances into the mirror, he wonders how he came about and what distant Englishman or woman is his ancestor.

Maureen, still frail, returns to bed while we explore Ajmer. Shah Jahan spent some of his time here, as did Humayun, Akbar and Jahangir. While Akbar built 'a palace', Shah Jahan, the flamboyant architect, scattered marble pavilions as carelessly as roses on the shores of Lake Ana Sagar. These exquisite pavilions, like exotic tents of marble, were meant for a great king to lounge on cushions, while being served wine by beautiful slave girls, listening to music, and staring out at the low Targah hills. There are four of these structures, around the same size, with marble walls yellowing like smoker's teeth, inlaid with flowers and leaves. They contain nothing now, except some graffiti and bird droppings.

As you stroll through them you understand the setting. It isn't merely the view; due to some geographical quirk, a strong constant breeze flows down from those hills and across the lake. The wind is strong enough for you to have to battle and the ancient trees growing in the garden have long grown misshapen, sloping away from the wind with tangled branches that remind me of flowing, carved hair. At the end of the promenade the wind is strong enough to halt you in your tracks and gulls, playing glorious and graceful games, stop their flapping and sweep past you like diving jets. Arjumand never saw these buildings, the grand

and casual gesture of a great emperor. Beneath the peepul tree there is a small plaque, attesting to our own careless disregard for the past. Lord Curzon, the man who restored the Taj Mahal in 1899, also saved these pavilions from decay.

Ajmer, due to its predominance of Muslim rulers, has two important mosques. Nalini can never resist popping into anything ancient and as we putter along narrow lanes, I wonder whether we will be permitted to enter. The Dargah mosque is situated in the midst of appalling slums. The street slopes down towards the entrance and the tiny hovels, as if in motion, seem to have crashed and crushed into one another. 'How sad, how sad,' Nalini repeats over and over again. 'I bet nothing has changed here for centuries. Why the hell doesn't our damned government do something?' 'Priorities,' I say sarcastically, unable to bear looking at our huddled poor. 'No doubt the MP for Ajmer lives in a great and grand bungalow and makes enough money for three generations.' We cannot but feel rage. The beggars crowd us, the children stare as if we are wondrous, the dogs sniff and eat in silted, black gutters. You might wonder why I now notice the poverty of my people. What about Agra and Aligarh, Delhi and Madras? Have I conveniently side-stepped the miserable poor, glaringly obvious to every tourist? The poor, like the sun and death, cannot be contemplated for too long. Gradually you draw the shutters, and only now and then, peering through the cracks in the blind when you are thrust into their midst, do you take note. Akin to love, it can break your heart—the waste of human life, the waste of intelligence, the waste of hope.

Nothing has changed since the conqueror Mahmud of

Ghazni sacked the city in 1024 on his way to Kathiawar in the west. Since its founding by the Hindu prince Ajaipal, invaders have been killing and sacking this place for centuries. Even Timur-i-Leng obeyed this protocol. The result now lies in the ruin of the people surrounding us: a hopelessness is etched in their faces, an air of dispirited misery mingles in the air with the odours of the gutter and cooking. I should think here, within the very genes of the men and women and children, embedded in their reincarnated souls, is a dark and depressing pessimism. Each time they hoped and rose and built and saved, a new conqueror sacked and pillaged, raped and destroyed. In time, they gave up and waited stoically for the next act of destruction, and they still wait, for time here is illusory. Fifty years, a century, and another army marches in. How can one get angry with a government swamped with countless similar pockets of poverty scattered so widely?

The mosque, naturally, is a magnificent edifice. We push and shove our way through the Muslim pilgrims and the bazaar within the high walls. The money changers call out as we pass, and merchants, no different from those found within a Hindu temple, offer cloth, silver trinkets, souvenirs, flowers, food, spices, beads, bangles. They offer the pilgrim all the gifts necessary to approach the tomb of Khwaja Muin-ud-din Chisti who was called Aftab-i-Mulk-i-Hind. (The Sun of the Realm of Hindustan). Since his death in 1256, this mosque has been one of the most famous shrines in India. The Mughal emperor Akbar would make an annual pilgrimage on foot all the way from Agra and built his own small mosque within these walls. In front of his mosque are two large iron cauldrons in which feasts, paid for by rich pilgrims, are prepared. They feed not the poor without but those working within. Further along, and I recognize the handiwork immediately like a true connoisseur, a marble mosque 100 feet long and graced with eleven marble arches. You can take it for granted anything of marble has been built by Shah Jahan. The floor is silken and cool under our bare feet and neither Nalini nor I can resist stroking these walls. Our actions do not disturb the concentration of the devout.

I read in one of the guide books that Hindus would not be permitted to enter any further but neither of us can resist the opportunity to peek into the shrine itself. We are drawn to the beautiful silver doors and the frame covered with horse shoes nailed on by horse dealers after favourable trading. To our surprise the mullahs beckon. With the queue we enter a marble room with jalis as walls. The crowd is shuffling in an anti-clockwise direction around a great square slab of marble. A shroud covers the tomb and the air is heavy with the perfume of incense and the sunlight filters through the jalis dabbing us with spots of light. Someone notices our bare heads and points. Nalini covers hers with her saree, I balance a hankerchief on mine. The shroud is being used to bless the people and on opposite sides of this square are two men lifting the edges and dabbing the bowed heads, and accepting donations. The first man dabs our head as we bow, and we drop rupee notes on the cloth. The second man attempts the same, but Nalini refuses a second dab. He looks a bit morose at missing out on the rupees for there seems to be a strident rivalry between the two dabbers. People behind us also dither between one blessing and two.

Outside the shrine, we sit awhile watching the pilgrims ebbing and flowing. There is a sense of orderliness, a contrast to the noise and chaos of a Hindu temple. After his investiture by his father, Shah Jahan came to this mosque to give thanks for his 'victory' over the Mewar Rajputs and his elevation to crown prince of Hindustan. Arjumand must have accompanied him here.

'Where have you been?' Nalini's son demands angrily when we return to the autorickshaw. This highly privileged child is surrounded by mute children his own age, staring at pampered flesh and the latest piece of Japanese magic on his wrist.

'I told you to come with us, but you refused. So don't ask where we have been.'

They bicker as the auto strains to climb back up the slope, once more passing the hovels and the goats sharing living quarters. India changes swiftly yet remains still. The flourish of technology, the flourish of industry dazzles us all. We have an abundance of food, an abundance of GNPs yet, like storms on a sea, we remain so stubbornly still deep beneath.

At the very top of the hill overlooking Ajmer is the Arhai-din-ka-jhopra (the hut of two-and-a-half days, from the myth it was built miraculously in that time). It has a peculiar history, which is yet typical of India. It began as a Jain college built in 1153 then the conqueror Mohammed Ghori destroyed it partially in 1192 and turned it into a mosque by building a massive screen of seven arches. Many a mosque in the north now was once the site of a Hindu temple. The Arhai-din- ka-jhopra is set well back within a dusty, deserted courtyard. A few beggars sit at the main gate and children play in the compound. The four or five storey high skeletal building, reddish in colour and yearning for its lost worshippers, is framed against a hard blue sky and brown hills. We wander around, trailed by the children wanting baksheesh, which we give, but as they miraculously multiply, we beat a retreat.

Our auto driver claims there is one more famous sight to visit in Ajmer before we can quit him. Winding back down these now familiar alleys, I know Arjumand too saw these same sights. She was, despite her station, a compassionate woman. There is a brief mention in the *Shah Jahan Nama*, the only little sliver of information on this woman, that she spent a great deal of time doing works of charity. The emperors too were generous in their disbursement of alms and at any celebration—for instance the emperor was weighed in gold on his birthday, and the gold was then distributed to the poor. All these efforts came to naught as yet another conqueror stepped on stage.

Nalini and I can't quite believe the sight we are seeing, a magical kingdom of gold and silver spread over the size of a basketball courts' and encased in a glassed-in room. We had been taken to visit the Jain temple and after receiving darshan from the priest, we had wandered out and seen a passive man sitting on a stool; obviously a custodian for something or the other. He collected a rupee and let us pass into a dark building and, unsure of what we were to witness, we had groped our way up even darker stairs. And then in a corridor, we glanced through an interior window and down below us was this city. It sprawls below in minute detail. Houses, palaces, a religious procession winding around the outskirts, chariots, elephants, camels, people and, suspended in mid-air above this strange town, a host of gods and goddesses.

'They look as if they're all of gold,' I pronounce with some authority. 'It doesn't look tatty enough to be papier mache painted gold and silver.' Nalini is doubtful. It would have cost a fortune to build, but in India such things are done for the sake of worship. The keeper of this phenomenon assures us it is all gold and silver, but naturally he would. I look up the guide books but find no mention of this place. Back in the hotel room, I try to describe it to Maureen. 'You could see the smiles on their faces, the muscles of the horses, yet even the caretaker couldn't tell us why it was made. It was as if someone had made it as an exercise, his obsession.'

It is enough to get her off her sick bed but when we return the doors are shut. I cannot resist showing her Shah Jahan's marble pavilions. She above all others understands my obsession with Arjumand and Shah Jahan. We stroll hand in hand in the twilight along the promenade discussing the emperor's whim to build these pavilions. We buy broken potato chips, hawked by a small boy. They are meant for the gulls that dive in the water after them. A man, gently deranged, coos and talks to the birds and after some hesitation they hop closer and grab a chip from him. On the lawn we watch youths playing a game of kabaddi. At dusk with the sky alight in pink and orange, and the sun a clear and brilliant red, the marble pavilions reflect the colours of the dying day. Gradually, they fade from sight until they are ghostly white silhouettes framed against a clear night sky.

The Scourge of God

While Maureen awakes robust, I awake fragile. It has nothing to do with food, but the weather. Ever since the long train ride to Udaipur without bedding, I've felt myself on the verge of a cold. And Rajasthan, being desert, can turn chilly at night and dry and hot during the day. In India we are not used to weather vagaries. The seasons are as fixed as a nail in the wall: heat, rain, heat, rain. If the rain and accompanying coolness should shift by a week, crops are destroyed, rivers swell and turn furious, countless human lives are lost in floods. On this day the sky is overcast. It has the dark, brooding look of a monsoon. The air feels uneasy, flicking dust and leaves into our faces. The monsoon season is over, but according to the weather forecast a cyclone is now raging over the Bay of Bengal and what we have overhead is the edge of that storm.

But we cannot not visit Pushkar. The lake, 8 miles from Ajmer, is considered one of the holiest sheets of water in India because of the confluence of many temples. As there is a Japanese youth, with a backpack and not a word of English in his vocabulary except a wide, charming grin and a vigorous neck that abounds with inflections, wanting to go out as well, we hire a van from the hotel to take us. The drive skirts the Ana Sagar lake, and through the gathering gloom we can scarcely distinguish Shah Jahan's pavilions on the far side. Soon the van ascends into the rocky hills. Boulders and the earth are the same dull yellow, like old gold and as useless for the stomachs of man and beast. The road is narrow and steep and thankfully the driver cannot practise any of his tricks as the van strains to take each curve and corner cautiously. The vegetation can hardly be described as scrub, but rather the mere survival of some dull greenish plant life, harsh and stiff, and even the goats find it unpalatable.

Pushkar is a village on the lake bank with the main road petering out at the far end, a few lanes straggling away to the right, a dozen temples and, to our surprise, a large population of European youths. They wander up and down the main street like countless Kims trying to blend into India. One, dressed as a Pathan, even deceives us momentarily as we stroll to the first temple, but it is all a fancy dress parade for these privileged children who spend an inordinate amount of time rolling joints in tea stalls, or else scribbling erudite thoughts in grubby notebooks. The temples fail to impress both Nalini and me. They are all 'new', built in the last two hundred years, some even more recent. In Madras, where our family worships, the Parthasarthy temple was built by the Cholas at least 800 years ago. But the foundations of these temples here are even older, only the structures now are modern. The Chinese traveller Fa Hien wrote about his visit to these shrines in the 4th century and described Pushkar as a magnificent town. But what we in the south take for granted, the antiquity of our architecture, eroded not by the sword but by weather and human neglect, here we are reminded that the Hindu was constantly under the subjugation of the Muslim invaders. The Pushkar temples were destroyed by Aurangzeb, in 1670. Aurangzeb was the third of Arjumand and Shah Jahan's sons. He was an intensely religious young man, a fanatic Muslim who took his role of Alamgir Padshah Ghazi (one who fought the holy war) as seriously as he did his other duties as Emperor. It is said that even during the midst of battle, he would dismount from his war elephant to pray (an action which often spread panic in his army as in those days if the King or General was not in constant view, his men presumed him dead and promptly fled the battlefield). He usurped the Mughal throne from his father, Shah Jahan, imprisoned him in the Agra Fort, executed his elder brother Dara, defeated another, Shah Shuja, who fled into the Ganges delta and disappeared forever, and imprisoned a third brother, Murad.

Aurangzeb's actions here and elsewhere continue to reverberate even today in India. The five Mughal Emperors before him grasped the one essential factor in the ruling of Hindustan: that this was the land of the Hindus and the very foundation of the throne rested on the acceptance of their rule by the Hindu. In pursuit of this tolerance, Akbar revoked the jizya (a tax on the Hindu) and his son and grandson followed suit. Although occasionally they would attack a temple, this was never a part of their political philosophy. The Mullahs looked on this tolerance with horror, and plotted continuously against the three kings at one time or another. Jahangir, impatient and capricious, imprisoned one of the Mullahs while Shah Jahan imprisoned the Mullah's son.

In Aurangzeb they finally found their champion, the Ghazi. He reimposed the jizya and began the systematic destruction of Hindu temples. The result was that one of the major supports of the Mughal throne, the Rajput princes, became alienated and Aurangzeb wasted years and a vast fortune battling against the once loyal Rajputs. Historians believe that if his elder brother, Dara, a religiously tolerant man in the philosophical mould of the great Akbar, had ruled, the present day Hindu-Muslim antagonism, including the creation of Pakistan may have been averted. Who can believe historians? They speak with hindsight. But Dara, pampered and loved, did not have the military experience to defeat Aurangzeb. The irony was that Shah Jahan made the same mistake with Aurangzeb as his father Jahangir made with him. He gave Aurangzeb too much military experience and when the brothers clashed, the warrior Aurangzeb easily defeated the intellectual Dara, and chopped off his head. The head, on a silver plate, was sent to the imprisoned Shah Jahan. This fratricidal act fulfilled the Mughal proverb: Takht ya Takhta—throne or coffin.

These temples in Pushkar do not possess the same brazen magnificence of our south-Indian ones; possibly in the intervening centuries the builders had forgotten their craft. We wander up the street, peering into one and then another, tangibly feeling the humility of an insecure religion. Maureen remains waiting outside each time. The frustration for her, and us, is that the bigotry of our Brahmin priests keeps her at bay. In spite of her being my wife, I have yet to budge these priests on permitting her entry. At the far end of Pushkar where the road peters out, is the only temple to Brahma in India. It was here that he is believed to have been incarnated. Brahma is the source of all knowledge and power, Brahma is the universe itself. The other two in the triumvirate, Shiva and Vishnu, have thousands of temples scattered over India and millions of worshippers. Brahma has only a few, and this temple is a small, unassuming modern building, with the symbol of the hans over the gateway. We climb the steps and peer in: a priest beckons, no one else distracts him. We pay a rupee and he murmurs a Shastra and we wander around but there is little here to attract us. We wonder what it had been like before Aurangzeb had razed it: magnificent, an appropriate abode for the creator of the universe destroyed by Alamgir (Aurangzeb's title) meaning 'the Seizer of the Universe'. Nalini shudders. 'What a horrible man that Aurangzeb must have been.'

Yet I wonder. In the last years of his life, he was desolately alone, totally paranoid about his own sons, embittered by his own bigoted actions, knitting shawls which he sold for charity, mourning the loss of his father's love. Aurangzeb wrote to his father: 'I wish to avoid your censure and cannot endure that you should form a wrong estimate of my character. My elevation to the throne has not, as you imagine, filled me with insolence and pride. You know from more than forty years' experience, how burdensome an ornament is a crown and how with a sad and aching heart, a monarch retires from the public gaze ...'

He died grieving and there is no majestic tomb for him. Akbar left an empire and great buildings; Jahangir, a curious sort of man, an intellectual, naturalist and a lover of fine paintings left behind great works of art; Shah Jahan left us the Taj Mahal and countless marble palaces.

Pushkar at this time of the year is quiet. In October they have a mela (fair) when camel and horse dealers descend on the village, and, between wheeling and dealing, race their charges. In November two to three hundred thousand pilgrims also flood the village for a religious festival. Now, we wander in the bazaar, Nalini and Maureen busily prodding and burrowing among the wares, in search of a bargain, in search of antiques. I find a battered silver hip flask with the inscription 'Captain A. Fowler' and by merely holding it my mind is filled with the adventures of an Englishman who, retiring, finally sold this to support himself in his last days. I want to buy it, but the price is exorbitant and the stall owner ignores my attempts to bargain. This occurs frequently now in India. Once I could haggle for days, returning weeks later to continue, because then the buyers were few. Now the stall owners know some rich European kid, dressed in his ragged fancy dress will snap it up. Or even Goldie Hawn, whom I am told regularly attends the November religious festival, but the mind boggles at this marriage between Hollywood and milling religious thousands. Or maybe, this too is part of Hollywood, the de Mille epic cast and Goldie Hawn fulfilling their different dharmas.

We gradually work our way back to the start of Pushkar and then find no sign of our little bus. I am sent to look for it while the women wait in the shade. But Pushkar is too small a place to lose a bus and I hitch a ride on the back of a passing cyclist. He is a keen youth, unsurprised by my request, who volunteers to search for this missing vehicle. On our return to the women, the bus has magically appeared but Nalini can't resist popping into one more temple, doubtless accumulating a lot of good deeds. To her delight, she finds it is a south-Indian temple with south-Indian priests and they bless her twice over at hearing their familiar mother tongue.

We wait in the bus for our Japanese companion and when after half an hour he doesn't show up I am sent off once more to search. I find him in a chai shop, contentedly sitting with the cyclist who gave me a lift. It seems a strange kind of meeting; they look as if they're old friends. How did they come upon each other and strike up so swift a friendship? The Japanese waves me away, gesticulating that he will stay the night.

Back in Ajmer, I inform the hotel about their lost guest and they accept his loss more equably than Maureen or Nalini. They both worry about this stranger wandering forever in the vastness of India without a word of English or an Indian tongue. We are booked on a late evening train to Jaipur, but with little further to do in Ajmer, I decide to move on by bus. I have seen where Arjumand spent her time here and for the last weeks, though I have stuck to her trail, I haven't as yet reached her most familiar route—down to fatal Burhanpur. In the bus station, I shove Nalini ahead of me into the long queue. With two women I have an edge over the other males who watch resignedly. The first man in the queue resists this queue jumper and he is roughly cursed by a small round man behind him. 'Can't you see it is a lady, you idiot. She has priority, allow her to buy the tickets.' 'But I have been standing here an hour.' 'Badmash, didn't you have a mother? Let her ahead of you.' Nalini, uncharacteristically, waits meekly as her champion pushes the man aside. He resists but the men behind begin to murmur, and the booking clerk is looking at him with disapproval. Finally, he wedges himself reluctantly against the railing, allowing Nalini to get to the window, and swiftly moves back to block my path.

Jaipur

The bus is not the luxury coach it claims to be, but it does have cushioned seats. The road to Jaipur first winds through fields of wheat—here and there we pass a camel caravan—and then great stretches of arid land. Running parallel with the road is a long straight snake of fresh dirt. It is only an hour later that I see the head of this snake: half a dozen Rajasthani women in their brilliantly coloured clothes are digging a trench for a pipeline under the supervision of a man squatting in spare shade. The women work in a calm unhurried manner. They remind me of an argument I had once with a bestselling American woman author. She was haranguing me from her lofty and privileged position about the tragic plight of Indian women. The Western woman's liberation movement, I pointed out, was based on the economic success of the Western economy. The Indian peasant woman is bound to harsh manual labour due to the survival level of her husband and family in a poor country. She would love to live in an air-conditioned home and gadget-filled kitchen and write bestselling novels but poverty forces her to work on building sites or digging ditches in the middle of nowhere. Ms Bestseller, whose fictional women were playthings for wealthy men, and I went round in circles all evening. She had a fixed image of the Indian woman and I had another: my sisters, my grandmother (a powerful matriarch), an aunt (a biology professor) and the economics of a poor country that bonded the village woman to labour and her womb.

About halfway to Jaipur a sign points towards Makrana. The road turning off winds through the barren land and disappears into a haze of rocky hills. The marble which Shah Jahan used for all his buildings, including the Taj Mahal, came from Makrana. In those days it was cut, blasted with gunpowder and carried on carts to the sites. Today that rich deposit of marble is used to line the walls of five-star hotels and millionaires' living rooms. It is a truly beautiful stone, pure white, flawless as a diamond, silken to the touch. The government, greedily awakening to this financial harvest, nationalized the quarries recently. The Raja of Makrana, whose family livelihood for centuries had been this marble, was thrown out on his ear. Even princes suffer the blows of injustice. By dusk we reach the outskirts of Jaipur and soon pass the pink fortress walls of the old city and disembark at the bus stop. Compared to Udaipur and Ajmer, Jaipur, the capital of Rajasthan, is a bustling, busy city. It is enormously popular with foreign tourists; only a half hour flight from Delhi, and you can deposit yourself in a prince's palace, and sightsee for the day at the other palaces before jetting back to Delhi. The bus stop isn't far from the Khasi Koti Hotel, once the Maharaja's guest house and now a state-run hotel. The Khasi Khoti is a serene, rambling building set in a large garden with peacocks strutting at the far end, and langurs playing tag in the trees. My cold, like the clouds overhead, has swollen and darkened. Nalini doses me with pills, Maureen tucks me into bed. I'm comforted by their concern and glad they get on so well together. Their relationship began with me as their bond, sisters-in-law, and over the years it turned into friendship. It was easy for both, as they admire and like each other. In Madras, they spend hours together painting or visiting friends and attending functions or just sitting out in the garden, talking.

And now they recede together from my drugged vision to explore the city but before I pass out, I manage a call to an acquaintance of mine here, Joey.

Joey is the Maharaj Jai Singh of Jaipur, the third of four princely brothers. I had met him the previous year and he had been a delightful host. Joey is the rare prince I like. He is a tall, shambling gentleman with little or no pretense to his princely heritage although his visiting card does bear his title, Maharaj—no 'a'—identifying him as a brother of the Maharaja. None of the princes are supposed to use their titles as Mrs Gandhi in 1967 de-titled all of them and also cut their privy purses. On our Independence, the princes of India still ruled their states, 600 in all, when Sardar Patel persuaded them to cede to either India or Pakistan. The ones who ceded to India were guaranteed this privy purse in perpetuity but the government went back on its word. The amount was calculated on the number of guns fired for them by the British. From twenty-one for the major princes: Jaipur, Baroda, Mysore, down to none for those tiny dusty principalities the size of a village.

My school harboured quite a few princes and I developed an allergy to all of them. They were arrogant, pompous children, spoilt, snobbish and quite unbearable as classmates. All were minor princes—Kolhapur, Sandur—and we even had a few sons of the Ranas of Nepal. Sardar Patel, an astute and intelligent politician who tragically died prematurely, called the Indian princes the 'gilded puppets of the Raj'. He was accurate in his summing up of their role. They were controlled and manipulated by their British rulers and those who rebelled were promptly dethroned. They were encouraged to play at swarthy Gatsbys and, during the early 20th century, they cut a flamboyant swathe through the salons of England and Europe; squandering their subjects' tithes on expensive gee-gaws—Rolls Royces and golden trains and magnificent parties. An acquaintance of my father, the Rajah of Junagarh, a tiny state in western India, once threw a wedding bash for his two favourite dogs. It cost millions of rupees and all the Indian princes attended the ceremony. The prince did give my father a gift we children cherished—a yellow labrador, one of the gentlest and most intelligent dogs we ever had. It came to us a neglected, frightened pup and finally died at the contented old age of sixteen. We called her Juno, in memory of the Raja and did her a disservice in the baptism.

My women (to be as chauvinistic as a Mughal prince) return from exploring the city palace in which martial history echoes in every room of the museum. Weapons of all kinds, fierce, barbaric, lie in great glass cabinets but there are also rare antiques, including a silver-plated palanquin. 'Of course the reason the Mughals kept attacking the Rajputs was to plunder their fantastic wealth,' Nalini sighs enviously. 'How I would have loved to live in those days.' 'You would have been ravished by a Mughal,' Maureen points out. 'Then maybe he would have given me a huge diamond or a handful of emeralds.' She waves the thought away. 'Anyway I would have committed jauhar.' And this certainly doesn't please her one bit. 'Jaipur must have fabulous wealth hidden away somewhere though the government didn't find even a silver ring.'

Some years ago, Mrs Gandhi ordered the tax men to search for this legendary wealth of Jaipur. They raided the palaces, and then took themselves off to the old one in Amber, and dug up every inch of dungeon and garden. All they found was an old cannon. This doesn't mean that Jaipur doesn't have its family treasures. It only means the government never discovered its whereabouts. The Jaipur princes were, if you listen to the Udaipur version of history, traitors. Jaipur was the first of the Rajput kingdoms to give their women in marriage to Akbar and throughout the reigns of Akbar, Jahangir and Shah Jahan, provided men and their own military skills in service of the Mughal emperors. It was finally Aurangzeb who broke the bond between Jaipur and the Mughals. But all this must be viewed in the context of the Rajputs themselves. They are divided not into castes, but clans, and since the beginning of their time on earth, they have fought and intrigued and abused one another. The Mughals were only a cause they used to continue their wars against their hereditary enemies—other clans. They formed alliances with the Mughals in order to battle Mewar or Malwar or Jodhpur or whatever. They never ever combined, as Rajputs, as Hindus, to meet the conqueror united, which made it all too easy for the invaders to pick them off one by one. They even sided with the British against Indian aspirations (for which the British made them favourites). In the Indian Revolt of 1857 the Maharaja Sir (the English flattered them with knighthoods) Ram Singh placed his entire resources at the disposal of the English to crush the rebellion.

In the dull limbo of my cold and a darkened room, listening to the edge of the cyclone that has hourly grown more menacing, I am forced to reassess my casual assumptions on the commonality of our identity as 'Indians'. Mere knowledge is not a strong enough glue when our history is peppered with so many betrayals. But this land of Rajputana is our equivalent to the Yorks and Gloucestors and Lords Somerset and Warwick, powerful princes fighting and betraying to extend their grip on power and territory. They were not Indians then but Hindus, Rajputs, and it is religion that binds but even this religion is filled with history. Legend has it that it was somewhere here in this state that the great battle of the Mahabharata took place. I cannot tell whether this epic is religion or history. They are subtly intertwined.

I wake the next morning, bogged deeper in my cold, with the strange thought of how my identity rises not even in history or religion. I am a river that divides India from Pakistan, that divides this country from the remainder of the world. The Indus gave us our name, as a people, as a religion, as a nation. But it was a name given to us by others, not taken on by ourselves. India, Hindu, the different interpretation of one rush of water. Why were we not called by our most sacred river for it flowed down from Shiva's head: Ganga,

Gangasthan. Is there another land, another people, another religion named after a river? I lie there all morning flicking through an imaginary atlas and can think of none. We are a most peculiar people.

By midday, my call to Joey is returned by his secretary. He has invited us to attend a polo match that evening. I had forgotten that even the previous year we had arrived in the polo season. The game takes place behind the Rambagh Palace grounds, and the women dress up eagerly in all their finery for this regal event. The evening is dark and threatening, spitting short heavy bursts of rain, and by the time we reach the polo ground behind the Rambagh Palace, we are all soaked and the game is well under way.

Joey's secretary, a plump, bespectacled man clutching files, leads us to the enclosure, waving aside another official's demand for a pass. The clubhouse has a stand above it, and we reverently take our places behind the old Maharani, Gayatri Devi, flanked by the present Maharaja's wife and other minor nobility, one presumes. Nalini is delighted at spotting her. She is the widow of the old Maharaja and was once considered the most beautiful woman in the world, and had her portrait painted by Pietro Annigoni. Unfortunately she also attracted the attention of Indira Gandhi. They clashed in the pursuit of power and Gayatri Devi, no match for wily Indira, ended up briefly in prison. 'Are you sure it's her?' Nalini asks after a prolonged inspection. 'Positive,' as it is impossible to ignore the centre of feudal attraction. 'Age hasn't been kind,' Maureen announces.

And here I shall avoid relaying the discussion on the faded beauty of Gayatri Devi that takes place in total disregard for the polo match in progress.

At the far end of the stand I spot her son (Joey's mother was the first wife). He is a sullen, spoilt young man with a whiskey-swollen face, and one glance conjures up the demons of my school days. I have met him a couple of times and each introduction, apart from a pallid handshake that made me wipe my palms, did not elicit a single word of response. Not even a polite murmur. Two chukkas have been completed, and it takes Maureen a moment to spot Joey charging down with the ball. The turf, normally brown and ragged at this time of the year, is green and plush. The horses thunder back and forth, and apart from Bubbles, Joey's brother, the Maharaja who keeps falling off, we don't recognize the other players. Polo is the only sport I know that is accompanied by a sense of worship, not so much for its athletic excellence but for the obvious display of wealth attached to it. Only the rich play it, only the rich watch it. The trappings here are certainly feudal. At the end of the game, there is a small prize-giving ceremony, and Bubbles' wife, a slim regal-looking woman, hands over a silver cup and medals to her husband and both the teams. When we adjourn to the clubhouse, Joey greets us with great affection and introduces us to Bubbles and his wife. 'Murari is a writer,' Joey announces enthusiastically. I receive the appropriate glazed expression that all writers receive in India. Bubbles and his Maharani murmur a polite response, before moving on. Thankfully, Joey doesn't introduce us to his young half-brother again. I couldn't take another limp handshake in my physical condition. Unfortunately, it seems I can't spend as much time with Joey as I'd hoped. He is dashing off to Delhi on the late night flight, but we arrange to meet for a drink in the Rambagh Palace later on.

The Rambagh has an impressive presence. In the glow of late evening, guarded by flunkeys now, its white marble glistens. The palace stands in a lush garden, and we glide through marble-floored corridors to the bar which looks out on an interior garden and fountain. The bar is an elegant, comfortable room. Joey joins us with a friend, Jayendra, a courteous, handsome man. 'What was it like living here?' I wonder out aloud to Joey. This massive edifice was once his home. 'I can't remember too much about it,' Joey says over a scotch. 'I spent most of my time in school, and was only here during the holidays.' He looks around, as if trying to recall a splendid lost youth. School for him was Harrow, England, as it was for his brothers.

With such little time at my disposal, I have no more time for idle chit-chat. 'When I was in Udaipur, they accused you Jaipur princes of betrayal by marrying your sisters off to the Mughals.'

Joey bristles. The feud is still alive, centuries recalled as if yesterday. 'You tell me—what did Udaipur achieve? They paid a heavy price for their defiance. Akbar razed Chittor and then the wars with Jahangir and Shah Jahan drained their resources. We realized early on that the Mughals were too strong for us, so by inter-marriage we saved our state and our people.'

'But didn't you give in too easily?' I too have been transported back to the 16th century, talking to Joey as if he were the then-ruling prince.

'We did fight them early on,' Joey insists. 'But then we had to save our state. They never asked us for tribute so we weren't impoverished by the Mughals. And don't forget, we fought fiercely against Aurangzeb because he was anti-Hindu.'

'Did the Mughals stay here?'

'Not here,' Joey says. 'This place, Jaipur, wasn't built then. When we lived in Amber, the Mughals would stay as our guests. But they didn't maintain a garrison in Amber nor did they interfere in our internal affairs. You have to make such decisions when the forces against you are considerable and you've little chance of winning.'

'Would Arjumand and Shah Jahan have stayed in Amber?'

'I'm quite sure, but not positive. When they moved towards Udaipur or going south, they would have stopped off in Amber.'

We kicked history around with time ticking by. Both Joey and Jayendra are Kachhwaha Rajputs and there will be no admission of fault, no betrayal. Although Indian history is one of constant betrayal. Then the country of 'India' did not exist, and princes schemed and intrigued for their own principalities

It's all the past, but the past never remains still. It stirs, flickers, slowly uncoils, repeating itself with monotonous regularity. Others were the foolish ones. Others defied conquerors. It is true. By cooperating with the Mughals their territories, palaces, and treasury were left untouched. They paid tribute to the Great Mughals and fought for them in bloody battles up and down the face of northern India—against the Afghans, against Gujarat, against Udaipur. In the siege of Chittor a Jaipur prince, a general in Akbar's army, must have taken great delight in the destruction of his ancient enemy.

As we lapse into silence, Nalini pursues her favourite topic of antiques.

'There is nothing left,' Joey says. 'It's all been stolen or sold. All you'll find are fakes.'

'In which case I'd like to visit the Murtis. Where are they?'

The Murtis are marble craftsmen, a special caste of Jaipur. 'Jayendra will show you,' Joey offers with princely magnificence, and Jayendra, princely too, graciously agrees to take us around.

Joey is running late for his flight and they both dash out but not before Joey insists that we eat as his guests in the hotel. It is a generous and casual gesture, and the maitre'd, used to such largesse from Joey, seats us reluctantly at a table and takes an inordinate amount of time to bring the menus. The agreement between the prince and the hotel chain must extend to free meals for his friends which could explain the sullen attitude of the maitre'd. He sees his profits dwindle with our appetites, and a swift slug of large scotch.

The previous year, Maureen and I had visited the site of a ruined temple at Galta, about 5 miles from Jaipur. Heavy rains had caused a landslide and the village boys were diving into a shallow pond and bringing up shattered pieces of marble idols. The temple itself, like so many in India, had a shabby air of neglect. Water had stained and damaged the murals and at the sanctum, a layman performed a perfunctory puja. Time and indifference were slowly glazing over this ancient site. The village boys surrounded us, surreptitiously beckoning to round-the-corners where they displayed their trove. The trove looked genuine and there in a darkened corner, I saw Durga. She was smeared with dried mud, sitting side-saddle on a lion and in her eight arms the weapons of war given to her by Shiva. I couldn't resist her, and a bargain was struck after some haggling and money swiftly changed hands. As I guiltily returned to the car, I consoled myself that I, and not a foreigner, had bought her.

On our way back from Galta that day, we stopped at a palace (owned by Joey's aunt) that was architecturally fascinating. Five levels, like giant gardened steps, led down to the bottom of a hill and we wandered through the deserted rooms with the chowkidar as guide who merely pointed to priceless pieces of furniture whose splendour even dust and neglect couldn't dim. Much later, sitting down to write a novel, this place returned to my memory. I remembered the shape: each room looking out onto a garden and below that garden another set of rooms. When I thought where someone like Shah Jahan, the great architect, should live, I stole this place and set it up in Agra on the banks of the Jamuna.

The next morning, Jayendra waited for us in his jeep.

'I am at your disposal all morning,' he announces graciously. 'Whatever you want to see here, tell me.'

'Only the Murtis,' Nalini says politely.

He drives us through the back streets of Jaipur in search of the Murtis. They live in narrow lanes with little room for a jeep, so we alight and stroll past the dogs and children, peering into dimly-lit houses. Like many typical Indian homes, these have a central courtyard. Men, women and children labour on marble, carving gods and goddesses with practised ease. Some of the carvings are small and portable, a few are massive. I stare up at a giant marble figure of Hanuman. His great tail curves like a lash behind him, and the head of the family proudly tells us it took a year to carve from one block of marble and that it is destined for a temple being built by an industrialist. It is quite impossible to imagine how they got this piece of stone into the building. Or even down the street. But Indian ingenuity is a strange and wonderful thing at times. Men, muscles, strained backs, sweat moved this rock from the quarries to this house.

That Durga I bought haunted me too. In the sunlight she smiled at me with the mystery of the Mona Lisa. It was the hint of a subtle curve in her mouth, the touch of a delicate chisel that had given her an air of serenity. I couldn't help but recreate her, chip by chip, later in my novel. I took her back in time, possibly she influenced my mind, bending it back further and further to the 17th century, when an acharya makes the long journey north to work on the tomb of Arjumand. I needed someone to carve the jali that surrounds her sarcophagus and conjured up Murthi. But if this great work wasn't enough, I wanted him to reveal his true talents, for he was an acharya, a carver of gods. And so, looking on this Durga I invented her from a block of marble and gave her to my Murthi knowing only his skill could fashion that smile, that calmness.

It is possible to tell a new carving from an old from the mere expression of a statue's face. Today, craftsmen are incapable of exactly creating the serenity of a Shiva or Vishnu or Parvati or Lakshmi or Durga. It appears we ourselves do not have an interior calm to be reflected in the stone we touch with our delicate chisels. A frozen grin emerges, a caricature, a kind of mask, which does not sit well on the faces of the gods but feels imposed.

Nalini is determined to buy a statue. We wander from house to house, until she sees a small Ganesh and falls in love with it. Having made her purchase and watched the creation of these pieces—the women endlessly polishing the rough stone until it turns silken, we feel we've taken up too much of Jayendra's time. Up till now, having spoken about his farm, we had presumed him a minor landlord. Before he drives off, leaving us by the Pink Palace, he hands me his card. As his jeep disappears into the press of streets and people, I glance down to find that mine host is the Maharaj Jayendra Singh, and I feel my memory of all those princely classmates has been shaken to the core. However, I console myself, as we wander up past countless tourist traps with their American Express signs, that Jayendra and Joey are the exceptions. The rule continues.

Nalini and Maureen are equally impressed.

'He really was nice,' Nalini announces to the street. 'We must write and thank him,' Maureen says.

We continue to stroll through this tourist Mecca, popping in and out more to please the women than to make a find. In one gloomy room with a gloomy old man presiding behind his counter, I spot a Mughal helmet. It is round, quite shallow and wide. It has a spike on top and in front of that two holders for the plumes. From the base at the rear flows a foot or two of chain mail. I peer at the tiny rings, but can't see whether they are covered with any writing, for in those days, inscribed on the rings was 'Muhammad', the incantation for protection. This one could have been worn by a Hindu warrior and I try it on for size. It covers my head like a loose basin as it was meant to sit on top of a turban. I decide to buy it. At the same time Nalini sees a low antique table, dusty and dirty, the brass plating worn and thin and the red paint faded. It is as if she has found the Holy Grail and the shopkeeper demurs at selling this priceless antique.

'It took me years to find,' he intones, 'and very few are left.'

'Is it genuine?' asks my eager, gullible sister.

The man looks pained. 'Of course it is a genuine Rajput table and I have been meaning to clean and repair it.'

Nalini cannot be dissuaded even by the logistics of our journey. We have miles to go still, countless train journeys, buses, cars, God alone knows what else, to reach Burhanpur. But she has to have the table.

'Well, you have to carry it then. I have no intention of lugging that damned thing around India.'

'I'll put it on my own head if necessary,' she sniffs, and the deal is done, money exchanged and already, as we climb into the autorickshaw, it has become a burden. But Nalini stubbornly clings to her table. I suspect if I pushed her to choose, we'd be abandoned on the road while she puttered off with her table.

My helmet, though awkward and heavy, is only a minor addition. I fondly imagine it on the head of one of my characters. Beneath the rust is brass work, so it certainly couldn't have been Shah Jahan's. His helmet and armour—four rectangular pieces of metal, padded on the inside and fitted so as to protect the chest, back and two sides—were all damascened with gold. A commander then, maybe even

General Mahabat Khan. I suspect it was an ordinary cavalry man who sweated in the heat, smothered by the dust of 10,000 horsemen, earning meagre pay for his services, and always hoping for the bonus of plunder.

But Jaipur itself was never seen by Arjumand. It didn't exist in her day. On her travels through Rajasthan, she and Shah Jahan would have stayed as the guests of the Maharaja in his palace in the city of Amber which was the capital until 1728. In the early morning light the view of Amber Palace is like an inaccessible vision. The building was begun by Man Singh I in 1600 and completed by Jai Singh. The yellow stone palace stands on a high ridge and cascades partially down the slope. A narrow zigzag road leads up to the massive gate set within fortress walls. Further down on level ground is a small lake surrounded by a beautiful garden with walkways between rose bushes. We all sigh in disbelief, wondering what it must have been like to have been a prince or princess in those days. They surrounded themselves with such beauty; their palaces and places were not mere fortresses, cold and sombre as those in Europe, but abounding with aesthetic harmony. Even the Great Mughal Jahangir envied Amber and to protect it from destruction in 1668, Jai Singh covered it up with stucco work. Our autorickshaw halts at the bottom of the road and tourists mill around waiting to mount elephants and take the ride up the steep cobbled lane to the entrance of the palace. Cameras whir and click as each poses in a howdah, grinning madly, waving, frightened too as the great beasts lurch slowly up the steep hill. We prefer to go on foot, and half-way our sense of adventure seeps away with the heat. But once within the palace, awe replaces our exhaustion. There are marble courtyards and corridors, muralled walls and mirrored ceilings, and again here plaster made as smooth and shiny as marble. We enter the Diwan-i-Aam and bedrooms and Diwan-i-Khas and it takes little effort to imagine the pomp and luxury of these princes. The air is not even disturbed by the tourists, rushing hither and thither with their cameras, seeing so little in their eagerness to mechanically remember this magnificence. We wander around a long while, savouring this princely atmosphere, the air deceptively still with memories. In the shadow of a gate that overlooks a gorge, an elephant, its trunk curled and resting on the earth, dozes. The mahout is stretched on the great back, asleep, lost in dreams of his ancestors. Like this too, in ancient days, they would have stood at this darwaza on guard, snoozing in the afternoon sun. Beyond the palace and along the hills runs a wall, broken and crumbled in places, and on the far peaks are watch towers. Below in the gorge is the ruined town of Amber: now a mere village with a great temple to Vishnu rising from its midst. Each time a prince was crowned Maharaja he came here to this temple to perform puja.

Arjumand

It would have been in this palace that Arjumand rested from the heat and exhaustion of her endless journeys criss-crossing the vast empire. As a princess of the empire, every whim and wish must have been looked after as she lounged in these cool rooms listening to music, staring out over those harsh red hills. It was not merely travel that exhausted her, but the endless stream of children that flowed out from her fertile womb.

Amber was but a stop for Arjumand and Shah Jahan on their fateful journeys south. With his success in Udaipur, Shah Jahan's next princely assignment was to subdue the Deccan. Every Mughal since Akbar had made this familiar commute and if they didn't make it themselves they sent a son. The rebellious Deccan simmered and erupted with monotonous regularity.

Once more Arjumand climbed into the carriage and our procession began its journey down to Burhanpur, resting a few days in Ranthambore fort on their way. However, our heroine, in spite of the discomfort of this trek, was to have no respite from the lust of her husband. The year after the birth of Dara she had her second son, Shah Shuja, and the year after him another daughter, Roshanara. And the following year came the birth of Aurangzeb. If we are to calculate at this point in time the total comes to six (in as many years of marriage), the first one having died at birth. There are others waiting: two more to live, to breathe the Indian air for years to come and six to gasp and expire. I wonder now, if those who had lived had died, and those who had died lived, whether the fate of India would have changed. For with the seven who lived, came death and destruction.

But that is not the story of Arjumand. She was the sacred cow to Shah Jahan's bull, producing child after child. But it isn't merely a tale of simple lust. It is a story of deep, deep love too. We must remember that as emperor, Shah Jahan was entitled to three more Nikah wives and as many more as he wanted. He could have married another three hundred by Mutah, and had as many concubines as his grandfather, Akbar the Great (5000, to jog one's memory). He was a man with a permanent erection, it appears. Instead, he remained lustily faithful to only one woman and even with the most ardent love, lust must wane, flicker and die after some years. With them, it never did. Their lust for each other appears to have gone on unabated until the very end of her life.

We now turn south towards this end. The next morning we catch the Jaipur Mail down to Sawai Madhopur, the station near Ranthambore. It is a dot on the map of India, but for the railways, a junction point. Here the meter gauge joins the broad gauge, the confusing British built three (narrow gauge) widths for our trains. Rajasthan glares and glitters into the dusty compartment. The land here is still desert, and the stops frequent. The stations are raised concrete platforms with a red painted room, railed in, and people climb in and out, regardless of side. As we move away from these isolated places, we can see paths leading away to the surrounding horizon.

'Where do they go?' Nalini muses. 'How far the poor people have to walk. I can't even see their villages.'

We watch them moving swiftly, an easy, mile-eating walk, that moves faster than this train. I watch one man for 20 minutes, striding through the shimmering haze, disappearing finally into a dip in the land, and still no sign of his village. I wonder what, if anything, has changed since Arjumand looked through the curtains of her carriage at this unfolding landscape; a bolt of dusty cloth lazily unfurled. Great armies marched and manoeuvred along this same route and the dust of their movement would have smothered the land, horizon to horizon. The carriage would have been hot and sticky and dusty and uncomfortable, but Arjumand was a woman of grit. If she bore these leisurely journeys without complaint, how much more fortitude did she show when she and Shah Jahan had to take to their heels in the not too distant future. When they had to race over a menacing landscape with the Mughal army in hot pursuit.

But this place we now come to didn't exist then. Sawai Madhopur rises out of the scrubland with all the harsh reality of an urban nightmare. It meanders out to meet us, while we and Arjumand are still enthralled by the desert and a great fortress, now abandoned (things do change, they do), which was a few miles back. Sawai Madhopur—such a lyrical name—is the true measure of India's industrialization. The carnage of our progress, our inexorable march to catch up with the Western world, lies cluttered here in the great heat.

A nowhere sort of place spewing up cement factories, small-scale industries, housing estates, and by the railway station, ancient locomotives lie gutted and abandoned like the bones of prehistoric beasts. It is a place to make your heart sink for here we have deliberately chosen to create ugliness, where once none existed. If only at times, the planners of these misshapen monstrosities, would take the time to look back, not on the West's industrial past, but our own. Here in this squalling township, we have made all the mistakes possible in town and home planning.

The town itself meanders along the highway, higgledy-piggledy, while the buildings are concrete blocks of the stale iced-cake variety. This is my own christening of modern Indian architecture. Each time I look at these buildings, I am reminded of the cakes with garish icing, collecting dust in the windows of bakeries. Whirling colours of pink and green and blue, prows and sweeps, curves and angles. The heat enters these concrete cakes and remains, trapped by this design to boil your brains out. Who, I wonder, are these planners and architects scattering monstrosities over the Indian landscape? They are certainly not sthapatis. According to the Manasar Shilpashastras, (5th Century BC but traditionally older) which anticipated Vitruvius, the Roman architect and civil engineer, by a couple of hundred years, high intellect and moral culture was necessary, and the sthapati 'should be conversant with all the sciences; always attentive to work, of an unblemished character; generous, sincere, and devoid of enmity of jealousy.'

The Shilpashastras detail the building of villages, towns and homes. The village plans were only extended for the towns of ancient India. The best site, after a careful test of the soil, was for the village to be built on ground sloping towards the east to catch the first rays of the morning sun. While the avenues would run east-west, the shorter cross-streets, to catch the breeze would run north-south. A temple would stand at the western extremity of the main avenue (Rajapatha, or King's Street) facing east, and at the centre at the intersection would be the Bodhi tree (Tree of Knowledge). The Bodhi was a banyan or peepul tree under which the council of elders would meet to discuss local affairs. But it also had a mystic meaning, planted at the centre of the cosmic cross, it was the Tree of Vishnu. The width of each road was stipulated to be 40 feet. Around the extremes of this rectangular village ran a road within the exterior stockade. This road was the mangala-vithi (Way of Auspiciousness). The village priests used it for their morning circumambulation. The village/town sentinels also kept watch here. This basic design could be expanded from 4,000 square feet for the smallest village, up to 30 square miles for a fair sized town. According to their calculations the rectangle length to breadth was one is to four. If at all possible, one of the long sides would face the river. The markets were not in the town centre but ran along the four exterior lengths of the village. The part which is least attractive, of course, is that the Brahmins lived towards the centre of this plan, and the other castes in descending order radiated outwards.

The Indian home too was built to a similar rectangular design, which can still be seen in the older villages. Four rooms make up the corners of a rectangle, with an open courtyard in the centre. Within the courtyard, there is space for the well and for the cattle to be penned in at night. I remember my grand-uncle's home in Vellore which had this style of architecture although no cattle ever entered. Apart from the use of the well, this style ventilated the building allowing the breeze to flow in and out freely.

As this is my second visit to Sawai Madhopur, I have learnt to avert my eyes from these eye-sores. I look beyond the railway station to the distant hills receding into the haze. Those hills are our ultimate destination and we all pile into the tonga—my sister caring more for her recently acquired table than for anyone else's welfare, including her own. The emaciated pony strains up the steep incline from the station to the flyover which squats over the rail tracks. I hate the strain on the pony and get out and walk alongside, in spite of the protests of the tonga wallah.'It's strong...very strong...' I do not believe him.

Fateh Singh Rathore

A year ago, while in Jaipur, I had mentioned to Joey that I wanted to visit a tiger reserve. There were two within reasonable distance of Jaipur: Sariska, back towards Delhi and the more convenient as our train for Madras would leave from there, and Ranthambore, more inaccessible, south of Jaipur and off the beaten track. Joey suggested Ranthambore, the old hunting grounds of the Jaipur princes, and promised to inform the Project Tiger director, Fateh Singh, of our arrival. He tried but couldn't make contact and we embarked hopefully towards Ranthambore. 'How will I find Fateh Singh in Sawai Madhopur?'

'Just tell a coolie, "Sahib Fateh Singh". He'll take you to him.'

We had then de-trained and to the first coolie, a thin, old man, more bones than flesh who heaved my suitcase on top of his head and then added Maureen's on top of that, I opened my mouth and pronounced that mantra: 'Sahib Fateh Singh'. He managed a cheerful nod, beckoned, and then proceeded to walk along the platform and straight off the end of it. 'Sahib Fateh Singh,' I called to him. He only walked faster along the railway tracks. 'Where's he going?' Maureen asked. 'All I said was "Sahib Fateh Singh". I didn't ask him to walk off the platform.' We hesitated, watching him pick his way over the railway tracks. An old steam engine puffed towards us, bathed us in steam and passed on. Our cases were slowly disappearing in a haze of heat. 'We'd better follow.'

Down we went, picking our way carefully through signal wires, discarded rubbish and train tracks. We caught up with him. 'Where are you going?' He grinned and gestured straight ahead. I saw nothing except tracks disappearing towards the horizon. He seemed to be heading up to Delhi, and I silently cursed Joey. Surely, he could have given me a different mantra, some other more precise direction to find this elusive Fateh Singh. A train came towards us, and the passengers stared in mute curiosity. We must have looked incongruous, a strange safari: a coolie, a bewildered Indian and a stylish blonde wandering along the railway tracks like lost urchins. We passed under the flyover, scrambled through some fencing onto a dusty road, trudged along that and then finally stopped at a rusted iron gate. 'There,' the coolie gave a toothy grin and pointed. On the rusty gate was painted the head of a snarling tiger. Within the compound was a bungalow. A couple of men, clerical types, watched us approach non-committally.

'Where is Fateh Singh?'

'Out,' one waved to the general horizon.

'When will he return?'

I received a shrug. There was a bench on the verandah and they suggested I wait. They took a look at Maureen and, moved to compassion, they directed us to a building in the rear. Inside was a bedroom, and bathroom. I left Maureen and the suitcases there, rewarded the coolie and took up my vigil on the bench—with an occasional foray to enquire into Fateh Singh's imminent arrival.

'Soon,' the favourite Indian non-committal reply.

I smoked and sat and wondered what I should do if this Fateh Singh never appeared. Catch a train to Delhi? Find Joey's summer palace? A hotel? Sawai Madhopur, squatting silently in the heat, didn't raise my enthusiasm. I really wanted to stay in the jungle, not merely visit and return daily to this exhausting barbarity of modern India. The decision was not up to me, but Fateh Singh. Joey had warned me he was an arbitrary man. I recalled Joey also telling me that Fateh Singh had recently been beaten up pretty badly. Joey had been vague on the details but murmured something about the local villagers ambushing Fateh Singh one night on a deserted road. His driver too had been badly hurt. 'Give him my salaams,' Joey had said, 'and say I hope he is better now.'

Half an hour, an hour passed. Cigarette butts piled up on the gravel. An open jeep roared into the compound and pulled up in a cloud of dust. A most piratical-looking man dressed in khaki shirt and trousers and desert boots with a sweeping kind of stetson on his head, very dark glasses and a fierce Rajput moustache (curving upwards like bison's horns) stomped past me with scarcely a glance and disappeared into an office marked 'Field Director'.

I leapt up.

'Wait,' a clerk ordered, rushing in with countless files.

Twenty minutes later I was summoned into the presence of Fateh Singh. His office was small and neat: a desk, his chair and in front of the desk, a row of straight-backed chairs. On the wall behind him was a large hand-painted map of Ranthambore. A clerk stood by him, feeding him files, which he glared at with his glasses at an angle, signed and pushed aside. At the same time, he tried to clean his ears with matchsticks wrapped with cotton wool. I passed him Joey's letter and took my place on one of the chairs.

Fateh Singh skimmed the letter, then stared up at me, blinking lazily, like some predator. The letter had had as much of an impact as a pea thrown at an elephant, and I suspected it had in fact not furthered my cause one whit. The questions now came quick and fast: what do I do? Why do I want to visit Ranthambore? What is my background? Why didn't I go to another reserve? I cannot remember them all but I do remember feeling that the questions were not so much for his information but telepathically for his animals out in the jungle. Would they, he seemed to consider, approve of my presence on their territory? I told him then of my father and my childhood, evoking the sympathy of government servants and a modicum of experience with nature, even if on a farm. He listened, but remained non-committal, signing blizzards of paper, and continuing to clean his ears.

Another supplicant entered, and sat by me. Fateh Singh transferred his attention. He knew the man and laughed a lot, but there seemed to be an undertow I could not decipher.

Fateh Singh turned to me. 'This man is a badmash. I sent him to jail for poaching and now he comes to ask me for a recommendation. I think I shall recommend he be returned to jail.'

I was beginning to like Fateh Singh, though the possibility still remained I would not make it on to the reserve. He was a flamboyant man, full of humour, and intolerant of 'nonsense', as he called it. He chided the man who then said he would go to a higher authority.

'Go to god, then,' Fateh Singh said. 'Ask him to sign your chit.'

The man left, and Fateh's attention returned to me. 'You can stay for one night only. I have other people coming tomorrow, and you will have to leave.'

It wasn't much, but it was acceptable. He jumped up, slapped the hat on his head, and marched out of the room.

'No baggage?' he enquired, and I realized I'd forgotten both Maureen and our cases.

'I have baggage and a wife somewhere back there.'

He looked nonplussed, then generously ordered, 'Bring her, too.' Maureen was lying on the bed staring up at the ceiling. She had the air of someone who had resigned her life to staring at this ceiling, and brooding on a destiny that had carried her to this room in a strange town, a strange land.

'Where have you been?'

'Waiting for Fateh Singh. He finally came and has allowed us to stay a night on Ranthambore. Hurry up.'

But wives kept waiting for hours are not wont to hurry. She moved in slow motion, while I picked up our cases and dashed back out. When I arrived panting, there was a young European couple standing by the jeep. They looked frail, tired, and had the air of people continually in transit. Fateh looked at my cases.

'Is that all? And where's your wife?'

Maureen strolled around the corner, carrying another bag. Fateh looked politely resigned, and we all piled into the jeep. The young couple, Claude and Clare, were French Canadians, and they'd been travelling for the last eighteen months. They had arrived in Sawai Madhopur the day before, but Fateh Singh had said there was no room on Ranthambore, so they had stayed in Sawai Madhopur and taken a tourist van trip around the reserve. On this day there was room.

Back to the present now.

This time, when the tonga pulls up in front of the building, Fateh strolls out and does a double take. He looks at the baggage accompanying us.

'Murari Sahib, you said you would come with very little luggage.'

'Fateh Sahib, all I have is this small bag. My sister owns the table and the remainder.'

Swiftly I pass the buck and Nalini glares at me and then mumbles her apologies to Fateh. She has, of course, heard my praises of this friend. Fateh peers at the table she had bought in Jaipur.

'That,' he says without a moment's hesitation, 'is a fake.'

'A fake!' My sister can't disguise her dismay. 'But the shopkeeper said it was very old.'

'Of course it's very old,' Fateh says. 'At least a week. Maybe a month. What, Madam, we have had so many conquerors coming in and going out, millions of tourists, and you expect to find one antique in some bazaar.'

Nalini stares at her precious table mournfully. 'Well, if I think it's an antique, it is.'

'Why not! It's all in the mind,' Fateh conciliates her and then pokes at my Mughal helmet. I hold my breath as he turns it over and over. Finally he nods approval. 'This is genuine. You see all this chain mail ... they can't be bothered to fake that ... too much time and expense for that. But,' as he puts it away, 'who knows? We're such an ingenious people when it comes to doing bad things.'

Chuckling, he has another jeep pull up and loads our stuff into that. Nalini, subdued momentarily, watches her precious table flung on the back of the jeep. We all pile into Fateh's jeep, and soon Sawai Madhopur drops behind. The air is fresh and cool for this time of the year and the sky darkening. The Aravalli hills loom out of the shadow: craggy, old, gnarled. Thorn bushes and twisted trees, boulders and shale, cling to their sides. Parts of them are rose-coloured stone, the same material used to build the Pink City of Jaipur. Fateh and I catch up with the news. Padmini, a tigress, has had cubs, more land has been acquired, his book on tigers (*With Tigers in the Wild*) has just been published.

But I have yet to tell you more about Fateh Singh Rathore, and how he was beaten up and left for dead. The event actually occurred four years ago though in the telling time, as it does in India, acquires a sudden immediacy. It began when Ranthambore was declared a reserve as part of Project Tiger. The 400 square kilometre area included a number of villages, and part of Fateh's job as Field Director was to shift the villagers out of the park and onto adjacent land. It was not to be an easy job although the incentives were decidedly attractive. The villagers were given a brand new village, a school, a dispensary, a panchayat hall, wells, and for every square foot of ground they owned in their original village, they would get that and half of it again; while those who'd owned no land would be given land. The cost of this move was to be split fifty-fifty between the State government and the Centre. The problem, however, was not the attraction of the incentives but something deeper. Ancestral property. It may be dried and useless land, but if it is ancestral property, it becomes precious. Even us urban Indians cling to ancestral properties, tarred, concreted, crowded, but if it came down to us through the generations, it has its own emotional value. It is our link with the past. Naturally, no villager would budge. The new village was ready, but no one moved. Fateh stopped friendly persuasion and set a deadline. Move or else... It was against this background that he was, one day, making his rounds in his jeep with his driver, Salim (who even now pilots us through the jungle, passing the ancient fort gate with the stream flowing to the left. The water emerges from the beautifully carved marble head of a cow). The villagers knew exactly where they could stop Fateh Singh. ('Betrayal,' he told me sadly, 'from within my own department. But why be surprised. We are a people who readily betray each other.') It was late at night when the jeep headlights picked out the villagers standing in the middle of the road. They were armed with sticks. Fateh stopped and got out. He knew their intention. 'What difference is it going to make if you kill me? The sarkar will just have you all imprisoned for murder and no one will look after your wives and children and care for your land and cattle. And after that, the sarkar will send another man in my place and he will do exactly what I intend to do and that is move you out.' One villager spoke: 'If we kill you, all this will stop.' There was no dissuading them. They attacked Fateh Singh and Salim threw himself over Fateh to protect him. When Fateh came to, hours later, the villagers had fled and Salim was unconscious. Fateh had a broken arm and leg and cracked ribs. He pulled Salim into the jeep and drove 20 miles to the nearest hospital where they spent a couple of months recuperating. When he recovered, Fateh plotted his moves carefully. He had all the authority in India to move the villagers. He ordered the police to climb the hills surrounding the village, and wait. At dawn, leading a convoy of trucks, Fateh Singh entered the village. He got down and pointed to the hills. Silhouetted against the sky, ringing the valley, were the police. 'Those of you who tried to kill me, will go to jail. But before that, everyone and everything in this village must be in those trucks by midday, otherwise I will order the police to start shooting.' Every man, woman and child, weeping and wailing, one old man clinging to a tree, every chattel, goat and cow, were herded into the trucks and driven out to their new village. Fateh then ordered the mud huts to be razed. The men who had tried to kill him were all sent to prison, and the villagers, now delighted with their new village, spread the word to the other villages. Fateh now has a drawer full of signed requests, on stamp paper ('otherwise they later say I forced them') begging him to move them to new villages as well. But, and there is always a 'but', like a hiccup, in the progress we make: the villagers still want to use the jungle to graze their cattle and cut wood, and Fateh has to be constantly alert they don't violate the sanctity of the wild life.

The jungle here is filled with ruins of the Ranthambore rajas, long evaporated into our collective amnesia. Langurs leap through the trees and silly peacocks race ahead of the jeep in panic before taking to wing, clumsily beating the air; filling it with their colours and their warning calls. We pass the steps leading up to the Ranthambore fort, and sweep up to the government guest house. The guest house, a single-storey domed building of pink stone, looks out across a calm, lotus-fringed lake. On the far shore, we can see herds of sambar and cheetal drinking the water, and the silent, barely visible ripple of crocodiles. Myriad birds dive into the waters or bob along, picking at the reeds. Immediately behind the guest house is a truly ancient banyan tree. It covers a couple of acres, and its branches support tribes of langurs and peacocks. The banyan, which never seems to die, is for me a grandfatherly kind of tree. It spreads and spreads its huge branches, broad and low enough for a child to reach, and makes an ideal playground.

Beneath this tree, over four centuries ago, the Mughal Emperor Jahangir once lunched on thirty-seven different dishes and then retired to snooze away a gluttonous afternoon in the summer palace, the poignant ruins of which now dot this lake, and two others deeper in the jungle. And a few years later, Arjumand and Shah Jahan too were wined and dined, lying on silken divans and watching the peacocks strut on the lower branches. Behind the tree rises a vertical cliff a couple of hundred feet high, and on top of the cliff, covering the whole crown of the hill, a few square miles, are the ruins of the Ranthambore fort/palace.

But I am in a hurry to enter the jungle, and so is Fateh

Singh. He sees it daily, and yet has never lost his love for the jungle and the animals. As we pass the lake, sambar look up at us from their feeding, and watch until we pass from sight. The dirt roads wind in and out of the scrub, passing more herds of cheetal, a solitary Nilgai, a couple of blue bulls, but the jungle also has countless birds. A quick eye can catch a glimpse of a mongoose sliding through the undergrowth, inquisitive nose sniffing at our direction, and the reticent wild pig galloping away in fright followed by her piglets. One of the summer palaces, with a chhatri, is supposedly the haunt of a tiger. We park by the waters, listening to the sounds of the jungle, but our tiger is not to be seen. (In the last census forty tigers were found in Ranthambore, and sixty leopards, but this count of leopards is a wild guess as they are a most elusive animal.)

'Maybe,' Nalini whispers to me, enjoying every moment of this experience, 'the tiger is a reincarnation of one of the princes.'

'It's female,' says Fateh.

'Then a rani,' says Nalini, undeterred. 'She has been reincarnated as a tiger and now comes to haunt her old abode.'

We wait a long while in companionable silence, comforted by nature. The fading sunlight turns the ruins pink and gold, but the magnificence of those princes still lingers on through the broken walls and creepers, and if one listens hard enough one can hear the voices of men and women laughing and calling, the voices of those ancient minstrels singing about the bravery of the Rajputs. (Fateh Singh told me a sound recordist stayed here for the night to tape the natural sounds of the jungle, and heard music and laughter but his instrument couldn't record the ghostly celebration). The irony is that what men took from nature, nature has now reclaimed. The walls of these ruins are pinkish, faded by time, the stones we saw in the hillside. Arches spring from the earth, only to tumble halfway back to the earth, and roofless rooms reveal the sky where once a princess sat and was waited upon by her handmaidens, who told her romantic stories of princes waiting for her.

Tiger, Tiger

On this evening, the jungle is silent. The edge of that cyclone sighs through the trees, birds swoop and call and the hum of insects lulls our senses. The herds continue to feed in the water, ablaze now with sunset's burnished glow. The calm is deceptive for us, not the animals. A herd of cheetal begins its approach to the water. You would think that with the other animals in the lake, this group of thirteen would be reassured. In the jungle nothing is assumed; karma choses one for dying. Eleven of the herd are bunched together. The two 'points' stand apart. The lead 'point' begins his/her slow approach to the water. Step by step, minutes of waiting, sniffing, looking. In a zoo the tiger is a brilliant yellow and black, but in the jungle, even feet away, he melts into the background of grass and shadow.

'It is safe,' Fateh whispers. 'It is safe, keep moving.'

But we do not have the same acute sense for survival. The 'point' deer, hind quarters bunched, takes another two steps. The eleven, giving him space, begin their move now. The back 'point' remains where he is, guarding the rear. The approach remains agonizingly slow, fifteen minutes, twenty, to cover 150 yards. Finally the lead 'point' enters the waters and one by one, distrusting even their fellows, the herd follows him in. But not the back 'point'; not for another five minutes. For all its power and strength and cunning, it's not easy for the tiger to kill. The jungle is full of alarms the moment he moves, spotted by the sharp eyes of one animal or another. First, the sweet, high call of the cheetal. It's both acute and nervous and quick to smell the presence of a tiger. And then, minutes later, the confirming bark of the sambar. This sounds like a smoker clearing his throat in the morning: a hacking, hollow sound. Because of its nervous anxiety, the spotted cheetal will often give a false alarm, a branch moving, a shadow playing tricks, the lingering smell of the predator. But once the slower-thinking sambar barks, you know the tiger is hunting. Then come the other alarms: the langurs boom and the peacock's 'mayur, mayur'. At night, the silent jungle can suddenly explode into a cacophony of signals and if you peer out at the black landscape you can 'see' the tiger moving.

The shadows of the hills stretch out across the lake and the jungle, mantling it with menacing patches of blackness. It is now but a few minutes to night and the jungle will escape us, swiftly returning to its true nature of lonely dying and living. Do all things, I wonder, revert: does the land revert to swamp once man has vanished from earth, do animals return, creeping out of their ghostly slaughter to once more stalk and hunt, and do ruins dwindle back, carved stone turning to boulder and boulder back to lava. For this is Kali Yuga, the last age of man, before the karmic cycle begins again. But that must be the point of beginning, in the slime, in the warm, humid rot of the jungle.

We have not gone so far back yet. Only a few centuries,

if one's imagination can restore these ruined palaces, hear the sounds of ancient kings, see Arjumand sitting on the palace walls looking down to the lake. She too looked on the face of this jungle, for the Mughals, in spite of their nomadism, followed well-trodden trails. But the peace for her here was deceptive. We see a gap of six years between Aurangzeb (born in 1618) and her fourth son Murad (born in 1624). It meant not tranquility but death; two or three or four children died in this period. And for Shah Jahan too peace was an illusion. Back in Agra the wheels of intrigue had begun to spin. The lovely Mehrunissa had taken too great a liking to power. Manucci wrote: 'she was a woman of great judgment and, of a verity, worthy to be a queen.' Being queen is addictive. She understood the limited nature of her power. Once Jahangir died—at the rate he drank it appeared to be continually imminent—that power would pass to Shah Jahan. Mehrunissa had to undermine the prince. It was not going to be easy. He had been granted permission to pitch the red tent and it seemed, for the moment, he could do no wrong in his father's eyes. Her first move to strengthen her base was to marry her only child, Ladli, to Shah Jahan's bastard brother, Shahriyar. He was the son of Jahangir's liaison with a slave girl and from descriptions, this Na-Shudari ('good for nothing') was an unpalatable creature. He suffered from a disease which caused his hair to fall out and his face to puff and peel. Poor Ladli was the pawn. Mehrunissa knew she had a better chance of controlling her daughter and Shahriyar, and the throne eventually, than her niece Arjumand. Of course, Shah Jahan read her intent as Mehrunissa had first tried to get Ladli married to him.

He was angry but had to move cautiously, cursing his half-brother for also becoming her pawn.

Arjumand was nobody's fool and as we saw, stubborn in her beliefs. Having made this marriage (even more sumptuous than Shah Jahan's and Arjumand's), Mehrunissa took the next step. She had Jahangir transfer Shah Jahan's hereditary jagir of Hissan Feroz to Shahriyar. She hoped this would provoke Shah Jahan into some action. It didn't. He simmered and protested but made no threatening move. He didn't want to provoke his father. The Mughal princes were insecure for the throne went to the strongest, and luckiest, son. Failure meant exile or worse. Shahriyar was now one step closer to the throne with Shah Jahan, moving down to the Deccan, many steps further away.

The jeep starts up, and breaks my reverie.

'I'm sorry Madam,' Fateh says to my sister. 'No tiger. She is refusing to show herself today. Maybe tomorrow you will see her.'

Salim begins a long circuitous drive back to the guest house. The evening has turned chilly and here and there where the road dips into a gully, we hit pockets of icy air. As we approach the guest house, Fateh signals Salim to stop quickly. 'Tiger.'

She is standing in another ruin by the lake, silhouetted against the sky, looking out at the darkening waters. The silence is eerie. The tiger turns to look at us and then returns to her vigil.

'There's your princess, Madam,' Fateh croons to my sister. 'There's your Rajput queen come back to haunt her old palace.'

'And she looks as beautiful as any queen,' Nalini says. 'I wonder what she's thinking.'

'Khana,' Fateh laughs and rubs his stomach. 'All she thinks about is her khana. She will wait in there until the foolish deer come back from the water.'

Minutes pass. To look on the face of a tiger, goes a Sanskrit saying, is to look upon the face of God. The tiger is the great wonder of Bhageshwar, our ancient symbol of power and magic and the unknown. But this most awesome and magnificent predator for me is another kind of symbol.

During British colonial rule between 1875 and 1925, 80,000 tigers had been slaughtered, and by the 1970s they were about to become extinct. Valmik Thapar, who has also written a dozen books on the tiger, despairs that it's already too late to save the tiger, and therefore our forests. In his recent book, *The Tiger: the Ultimate Guide,* Valmik quotes a stanza from the *Mahabharata*: 'Do not cut down the forest with its tigers and do not banish the tiger from the forest. The tiger perishes without the forest, and the forest perishes without its tigers. Therefore the tiger should stand guard over the forest and the forest should protect all its tigers.' There are conflicting reports on our forest cover. The government claims it's been increased to 33 per cent from 20.5 per cent, while others claim our forests are shrinking due to encroachment and degradation. Cynically, because of our exploding population and exploding development, I believe the shrinking statistics. I have a built-in antipathy towards the Chinese. Over the years I had written, in my column, that the tiger is vanishing into the greedy mouths of the Chinese who believe that the tiger's penis, bones, various parts, are a powerful aphrodisiac. I had hoped Viagra would have saved the tiger but obviously the drug hasn't yet reached China. The Chinese also kill elephants for ivory and their skins, and rhinos for their aphrodisiac horns. Clearly, the Chinese need help with their sex lives.

This act of conquest was the symbol of subjugation, not only of Bhageshwar but also of a land and of a people. Not far from where this tiger sits peacefully, is a cliff face. A tiger was driven against the face by beaters and their highnesses the Maharaja of Jaipur and the Duke of Edinburgh gunned it down from the safety of a howdah. Then even more recently in 1979, when Fateh Singh was transferred from Ranthambore, the Indian government gave permission to a foreigner to shoot a tiger. He set up the bait of a live goat and two tigers came. He killed one and wounded the other. Fateh Singh returned then and, weeping, went out with his rifle to kill the wounded tiger.

But I cannot apportion blame only to modern times. The Mughals brought their own method of hunting down from the steppes of Asia. Timur-i-Leng invented the qamargah (enclosure) with the use of a large army and his descendants remained loyal to tradition. It was used to practice military training. The soldiers, many thousands, would form a huge circle and drive the animals within that to a central point. In one hunt in 1567, the diametre of the circle was 60 miles and 50,000 soldiers, over a month, gradually closed the circle to 4 square miles, driving the animals towards the centre. Once the prescribed size was reached, with the great uproar of tigers, cheetal, panthers, sambar, the emperor would enter the arena, along with chosen courtiers, but he alone, armed with bows and arrows, or sword and shield, maybe a musket, made his kills. Akbar once even used only a lasso. As the circle tightened, it became impossible to keep the animals penned and they would break through the human chain. Later, wattle screens were used in place of the chain. Paintings depict Akbar fighting tigers with a spear and shield, and according to legend in one qamargah he was wounded in the genitals by a sambar. The delicate wound took six months to heal. An emperor would hunt for five days and once he had was sated, selected noblemen took their turn. Naturally in such a dangerous chaos of men and animals, a few scores were settled, according to Abul Fazl, Akbar's biographer. After the nobles, the soldiers took their turn. And even women, including Mehrunissa, would hunt in the qamargah. Once the soldiers were satisfied, holy men would plead for mercy for the animals still within. Once, before he went into the qamargah, Akbar had a mystic vision and ordered all the animals to be freed. However, his descendants continued with this traditional hunt, as it was a substitute for war for those taking part to see who was the bravest or the biggest coward. After a day's hunt, the emperor and the entire Mughal court would retire to feast and drink the night away. At least in this one-to-one combat the odds were, if not even, fair enough.

I will always remember my first glimpse of a tiger here in Ranthambore. It was on our previous visit. Maureen and I had set out at dawn with Fateh and we followed the trail of pug marks on the road (tigers prefer dirt roads because of their sensitive pads). The jungle at dawn is gray and ambiguous, shadow and light look the same, there's a uniformity that baffles the eye, but Fateh's eyes are sharp and quick. He suddenly pointed to the shadows, and at first I saw nothing. Then, like a puzzle emerging, we spotted the tiger. He was standing stock still, the striped coat blending in with the subtle shadows. He was 20 yards away and concentrating fiercely on something just beyond our line of vision. Suddenly, a fawn broke away. It leapt through the bushes, spurted across the road and bounded up the slope towards its herd, which was also tensely watching and waiting. The tiger bounded, accelerated and then in the road, braked, and wistfully watched the herd bolt, calling frantically. Then he turned to look at us. He was full-grown and magnificent with a massive head. The yellow slanting eyes watched us with a strange benign stare; like an old and wise man, hinting with a flick of his tail his exasperation at our presence. At 10 feet, this symbol of god filled me with awe. I had not known what my feelings would be when I saw a tiger in the wild, and so close. Fateh Singh had said a famous English journalist had crawled on to the floor of the jeep at his first sighting, for Fateh never carries a weapon, nor does he allow anyone else to. I wanted to approach this mesmeric beauty, such power, such perfection, such proportions. The languid ripple of muscle, the arrogant face. A foolish wish for this creature could have removed my head with a sweep of its paw. There is a legendary story about the Buddhist prince, Mahasattva, who while riding out in the jungle saw a starving tigress with her cubs. Moved to compassion by her plight, he fed her his own body.

My feeling is not that magnanimous. This crazy need to climb out of the jeep is the natural acquisitive impulse of man to possess. We have to possess beauty and this act of possession is the seed of this animal's destruction. If it were ugly and misshapen, it would live on forever, but its beauty is our magnet, its power the attraction. And we have to possess, for that is our nature. Conquer, cage it, kill it, hang its skin on the wall or lay it on the floor so we may walk on it and in this act of desecration, prove to ourselves, our admirers, that we have a greater beauty, a greater power. Possession is merely destruction.

The tiger remained regal, poised, staring into the lens of my camera (and this insane act too was possession. I needed to carry away his spirit in this little black box and flaunt him to my friends). Then he turned and stalked off down the road. We followed him down the road. After a glance behind, tiring of our persistence, the tiger moved off into the jungle. Watching it pad through the shadows, I became suddenly aware of its true nature: the power to frighten. It was like watching a cyclone, a force greater than man too, rolling through the undergrowth, flattening all in its path: cheetal and sambar called frantic warnings and stampeded up and down the slopes, madly leaping over nullahs and rotting trees, langurs climbed higher and higher, chattering in fear, sending out their booming calls to the jungle, peacocks clumsily took to the air, sending out their 'mayur, mayur' calls, smaller birds, panicked, took to the gray skies. Nothing could ignore the presence of the tiger. Nothing could remain at peace while he passed. And when he had moved on, a sigh swept the jungle, even the trees and grass seemed to droop back in relief, and normalcy returned. Death came another day, in another place. In this other place now, nothing occurs. Our tiger, behaving like a reincarnated princess, slips away to another room and fades from sight. We release a collective sigh.

'Tomorrow, Madam, we will find you more tigers,' Fateh promises my sister, even as the first light spit of rain touches our faces.

Indira Gandhi, the patron saint of the tiger, championed the cause of Indian wildlife and legislated ten other similar reserves scattered across India. Their survival in the delicate ecology of India's economy is fragile. The pressure on these pockets of natural wildlife is not merely population but the basic needs of our villagers. They need grazing land for their cattle and goats and with the price of firewood, a small bundle costing fourteen rupees, fuel for their cooking fires.

'We have to educate our villagers,' Fateh tells us on the drive back to the guest house. 'We have to not only teach them about the importance of wildlife but provide them with alternatives for their basic needs. We have to subsidize them to stall feed their cattle and provide them with a cheap fuel. Only then will they leave the jungles alone. Another problem are these damned tourists. They demand the right to look at the animals and they're constantly in and out of these places, disturbing the animals. The government must deny this right. The animals should be allowed their peace, otherwise they get so tame they'll start eating out of your hand.'

Even though I am certainly guilty of tourism, I have to agree with Fateh. Even within a year, we've noticed the increase in jeep and coach traffic, crammed with sightseers, criss-crossing the reserve. I'd earlier cracked that Fateh should set up traffic lights and had received a sour glare.

But they are not his sole problems. The politician too interferes. A day or two before, a State Assembly man had announced in the house that, 'Fateh Singh dresses up his trackers in tiger skins because there are no tigers in Ranthambore.' Fateh merely rolls his eyes but it means a trip up to Jaipur to answer this accusation.

'Oh, they are such fools,' Maureen remarks angrily, for Ranthambore and Fateh are dear to her. 'Are they really that stupid? Don't they have anything better to do for India?'

'Bloody bastards,' my sweet Indian sister chimes in. 'Why don't their idle minds turn to eradicating poverty in Ajmer?'

Having aroused the ire of my women, Fateh retreats to his room. We are served the Ranthambore chai—tea with cloves and cinnamon—on the balcony overlooking the lake. The opposite shore is barely visible and the sky is as swollen with clouds as my head with the damned cold.

'He and Ranthambore remind me of Nayana,' Nalini suddenly says to me.

I'm not surprised this place and the man should evoke our father. There is, in spite of distance and age, a similarity. Both government servants, both fiercely protective of their preserves, both honest men, both with dreams of bettering India and, if Fateh is to follow my analogy further, he too will fail. India is difficult to change. Men with strong hearts stumble and fall against the machinations of men with avaricious hearts. As my father loved the farm on which we spent our summers as children, so Fateh Singh delights in this place. Ranthambore is his first and only love, and although he has spent time on other reserves—Sariska, Bharatpur—he has always returned to Ranthambore. He has even turned down promotions to remain here, a rare quality in a government servant. The price he pays is his separation from his wife and family. But the Fateh Singhs in India are few. Even as his years speed by—retirement at fifty-five—there are none with the same care and concern to look after Ranthambore. His subordinates prefer to live in Sawai Madhopur rather than the jungle, preferring the bright lights to the brooding darkness of the land. But that is a minor failing. On other reserves, corruption is rampant. Sandalwood trees are allowed to be felled, whole forests sold away for the kick-backs. While down in the south, the forest department turns a blind eye to the most savage poaching of elephants ('Listen, sir,' I was told, 'the politicians are in the pay of the poachers'). A hunter I met told me blandly that for a substantial bribe he could shoot tigers galore. So survival here, for these tigers and leopards, sambar and cheetal and nilgai, for jackals and vultures, for the langur and the great kites, becomes impossible.

As if on cue, waiting in the wings of the guest house for these thoughts to pass and for the rage to subside, enter Valmik Thapar and Tejbir Singh, a languid duo of filmmakers. Valmik is like a bear, shambling, bearded, overweight and withdrawn; Tejbir is slim and silent. It turns out they are also brothers-in-law; Tejbir having married Valmik's sister. They collaborated on the book with Fateh and for the last five years have been shooting a documentary on the tiger.

It will one day be priceless, our celluloid memory of the great Bhageshwar.

The distant shore has faded from sight, the wall of darkness creeps up on us. A hurricane lantern is placed on the table, barely illuminating our faces. The hills across the lake, silhouetted against the sky, resemble a woman lying on her side. The curve of her head, shoulders, waist, buttocks and finally her ankles taper away into the darkness.

We hear a car pull up, and three government officials join us. One of them, the collector, appears to be a young man. The only distinguishing feature is the stetson on his head. The others are a woman and a middle-aged man. Their faces remain in darkness and our conversation is desultory until Fateh materializes, clutching a bottle of whiskey. His evening ritual is rigid and enjoyable, a couple of burrah pegs, good conversation and finally dinner. Last year, we had spent an inebriated evening with a Deputy Inspector General of police. The company this evening is not that exalted, and after a few drinks the topic turns to Rajasthani folk songs. Fateh sends a servant scurrying for one of his trackers. The man joins us with his flute and Fateh sings duets with him. Their voices fill the air, fill the jungle night, rising up to the dark, silent palace behind us. Do those ghostly princes listen to the songs about their valour sung by these Rajput descendants? No doubt, Arjumand and Shah Jahan, high up in the Ranthambore fort, must have also looked out on this jungle.

At nine with the serving of dinner, the evening comes to an abrupt end. Whether in fashionable Bombay or jungley Ranthambore, it is the signal for guests to depart or retire to bed. Maureen and I remain on the dark balcony, feet up on the railings, staring out at the black void in companionable silence.

Like me, she too spent some part of her childhood on a farm. An electricity-less world is the memory of our childhoods, and this brief return to the vastness of night is a familiar feeling. It's good to escape from its seductive distractions, for electricity, above any other invention, has divorced us from nature. It separates us from the heavens, separates us from the land and the waters and the animals, it turns us inwards, trapping us within brightly-lit, warm cells. We turn our backs on the natural world, with its power to make us wonder and to frighten us into a sense of mortality and insignificance. In the old days, even lamp light was a distraction to the minds and thoughts of men. Our ancient rishis would walk miles away from their villages in order to escape their glow and then, lying on the ground in a remote field, they would study and map the movements of the stars and the course of our philosophy.

The jungle around is silent and the stars hidden by the fleecy clouds. Then, to remind us of its own truth, far away and faintly, we hear the warning call of the cheetal. It comes once, then fades, comes once more, stronger. We wait and then louder, and more urgent, the confirming bark of the sambar. The bark is repeated once, twice, thrice, and then the silence returns suddenly. A tiger has made a kill.

We are up early at dawn and Fateh too had heard the calls. We spend the next few hours roaming the jungle in his jeep, looking for pug marks and the kill but Bhageshwar remains elusive. We breakfast under the banyan tree in the spiritual company of Jahangir and Shah Jahan and Arjumand. We also have more earthly companions, the langurs and peacocks. They circle our table, avid for toast. The silvery langurs are led by a fierce and moth-eaten rhesus. (Fateh: 'They are like us Indians. We allow aliens to rule us.' The jungle has more than one metaphor). The bold rhesus suddenly leaps forward and snatches Maureen's toast. To his surprise, she grabs it back. He takes another swipe and they tug at it until it breaks, and he leaps back into the banyan, scolding angrily and being scolded too by my wife.

Fateh's mornings are spent in Sawai Madhopur, signing his files, and we climb the steep, rocky pathway up to the deserted Ranthambore fort/palace. It was built around 900 AD but no one is very sure of its exact age. Its last princely inhabitants, 400 years ago, were the Chauhan Rajputs. Fateh, who has explored it thoroughly, thinks it is older as it is a blend of differing architectural styles, some from an earlier time. As it passed from conqueror to conqueror the place subtly changed shape. The sun is hot on our backs as we climb and we pause for breath at every zig and zag of the pathway. The way up is easily defensible. It passes between high walls and under portals and is never wide enough to take more than four horsemen abreast. It was meant to be invulnerable and was yet so vulnerable to patient armies.

It fell the easiest to Akbar, a year after he conquered Chittor. He did not need to build a sabat or mine the sheer cliff face, nor squander the lives of countless men. He appeared with his vast army on the plain below and merely huffed and puffed, and the gates of Ranthambore flew open. His destruction of Chittor taught a terrible lesson to those who wanted to defy him—he was implacable and ruthless. But once he entered here, he returned the fort to its prince and took a few women as wives to seal a diplomatic agreement. Ranthambore then became a stop-over for all the Mughals on their way south to Burhanpur, and this included Shah Jahan and Arjumand. Within the final portal where a soldier once stood on guard duty in a large niche, a man squats beside an earthenware pot. 'Pani,' he murmurs enticingly and in exchange for ten paise he pours sweet, cold water into my cupped palm. I drink greedily. 'God knows where that water's come from,' Nalini warns but our thirst is too great and has to be quenched. Though only a few travellers pass this way, I cannot help but admire the enterprise and the optimism of this man.

We step into silent sunlight. Broken walls and fallen pillars lie scattered amidst the undergrowth. The jungle below has lost its identity and appears only as a gray, ambiguous mass of vegetation spreading out to the horizon. It has leapt up the cliff face too and entered here. Little footpaths wind through the thorn and ruin and maidan. A chhattri stands in desolate reminder of a prince and beside it is a low, gloomy place of worship. Goats skitter away from us as we descend down a road, while above us, on the battlements a tribe of langurs chase each other up and down. At the bottom of this road, hidden by the ruin of a temple, is a clear tank of water. A man squats on the far side beating his clothes. What remains around us was once the residence of the prince. The town itself, beyond these ruins, has dissolved into dust and the jungle has erased all memory of it. Taking another path, we come upon a great rectangular building. It has an air of solitary grandeur and we presume it to have been a palace but we cannot enter. The department of archaeology has beaten us to it and locked the doors. We peer through cracks in the ancient warped wood and only spot pigeons strutting over dusty floors.

'How sad, how sad,' Nalini murmurs and her words infect us with melancholy.

As a people, our collective memories of this place are blank. How did they live? How did they behave? What were their names? Whom did they love? The past here has no resounding echo; there is no sound lingering for us to hear. But we have no time to mourn. I know that ahead of us still on this voyage will be other forgotten pasts, other ruins, other ghosts tugging at our hearts.

It was not war that finally destroyed Ranthambore, but population pressures. The land below could not support the people, in spite of the man-made lake, and so the people slowly drifted into the village that became Sawai Madhopur. Soon, the king saw no one to rule and he too abandoned the palace to the goats and monkeys and snakes and deeper into the hill the panther watches all like a patient ghost waiting to visit death on this place once more. At the gateway to this fort stands a granite carving. It is shoulder height, oval and a few simple lines chiselled on the smooth stone have turned it into the serene and smiling face of a woman. I take a photograph of Nalini and Maureen on either side, a tourist kind of shot, but it is later when the photograph is developed that I note the haunting similarity between my sister and this stone mask. The eyes and mouth are the same, and it could have been her posing for this forgotten sculptor. Do we, reincarnated time and time again until we achieve moksha, resemble the original prison of our souls? Looking on this photograph the past, though blurred, has strangely materialized in human shape.

'I told you I'd been a princess,' Nalini comments complacently.

But the sky has begun to darken, and though it is only noon, twilight descends. We return to the guest house to sit on the balcony, wrapped in quilts for the afternoon has turned cold. As we stare out across the lake and the hills we suddenly see a dark line approaching us from beyond the horizon. It's as if a giant pencil, with swift strong strokes, is shading the sky. The line reaches the far shore of the lake before we realize we are watching the front of a huge storm. In a city, behind and beneath walls and roofs we don't see the advance of cyclones and storms. It merely rains. But this is mesmeric, we can actually see the advance line by line. There, halfway to us ... the waters of the lake dimpling, churning, waves rising, and then it hits the bungalow. Great sheets of water sweep over the balcony, drenching us and we scurry for the shelter of the rooms. For an hour we watch the storm, bending palm trees, snarling and snapping off branches, blowing birds across the sky like tissue paper and enraging the once placid waters of the lake. Then as suddenly as it came, it has passed on, watering the parched earth, flattening ripe corn, filling nullahs, swelling rivers. The air has that fresh odour of newly turned earth, and the sunlight glistens on the flanks of the hill. The morning newspapers will report the deaths and damages of its fury.

The film-makers, Valmik and Tejbir, look out mournfully

as if grieving, but remain silent. When Fateh stomps in, delayed by the storm, we learn why. He too stares out at the jungle with a similar expression.

'No more trips in the jungle,' he announces. 'The roads will be impassable. Two years ago I was out in the jungle when a storm came and I had to abandon the jeep and walk back.'

'How long before we can go out again?' I ask.

'A few days. But that depends on whether it rains again.'

We break out the whiskey early as a consolation and listen to Fateh spinning his jungle stories. The weather doesn't clear and at night I hear the intermittent downpours. But between the whiskeys and heavy doses of vitamin C, I wake the next morning with a clear head. It rains most of the morning and we begin to feel like prisoners. The jungle is mired and even the warning calls now have totally ceased.

It's time to move on and I check the train timetable. We can catch either the Frontier Mail or the Dehra Doon Express going south. Neither, however, stop at Indore. We'll have to change to a local train at Ratlam. When the rain breaks, we pile our luggage into the jeep. Nalini reverently wraps her fake table in an old saree. Bedraggled langurs and soggy peacocks watch our jeep slip and slide over the muddy road out. Even in such a short time, the colour of the jungle has begun to turn from its drab gray to an exuberant, new green. In a week, it will look as brilliant as a billiard table.

But halfway into Sawai Madhopur, the rain starts again and Salim, afraid of dissolving, races like a truck driver. A joint scream and scolding from my women calms him down and we reach Fateh's office soaked. Sawai Madhopur looks as unappetising as ever, and we feel as if we've woken from a dream into dreaded reality. We had forgotten the chaos, the press of humanity, the ugliness of man's creations.

As the Frontier Mail isn't due for an hour, we wait in Fateh's guest room with his seventeen-year-old son Govardhan. We had met him briefly in the jungle guest house. He's a shy, slight boy with ambitions to become an artist and his sketches of the jungle and a few of his father are really good. But we cannot follow our dreams that simply in India. It's too frightening for, like my artist-waiter on the Grand Trunk Express, Govardhan knows he cannot survive.

'Baroda has a good fine arts school,' he confides, wanting encouragement. His life has been spent in the ex-princely boarding school of Mayo in Ajmer and he lives with his mother and sister in Jaipur. The strongest resemblance to Fateh is the curling moustache.

'I advise him to do medicine,' Fateh interjects. 'Then he can do art, he can paint to his heart's content.'

'But it won't be easy,' Govardhan says. 'It will cost a lakh to get a seat.'

'That's more expensive than the south,' Nalini says. 'There a seat will cost you 20,000 rupees, but I hear in Hyderabad it costs fifty.'

They are not matter-of-factly discussing fees, but bribes. The better a medical or engineering school, our two staple professions, the more we pay for our privileged child to be admitted. It is an accepted way of getting an education. Our youth has long been disillusioned by this corruption. They know, no matter how brilliantly they perform in school, their only chance of entering a professional course is for their parents to bribe the university. 'It's not only university,' Nalini interjects. 'Even to get your child into a decent school, even kindergarten, you have to make a "donation" of five or ten thousand rupees. All along the way we have to pay and pay.'

'A boy can be a total idiot,' Govardhan warms to the subject for since finishing school it has been his sole preoccupation, 'but if his parents can buy him a seat, he'll get in. And then he doesn't have to study too hard. He can bribe the masters for his question papers, and do you know what some authorities do? They'll switch the marks. A poor boy's excellent marks will be switched for the rich idiot's marks. And what can we do? We can't prove it.'

In this swirling world of high finance the poor do get a look in. Every school and university has to allocate seats to the under-privileged and minorities—'scheduled' castes or tribes, Muslims, Christians—and often it is easier for them to enter this heaven than a non-labelled boy or girl. But survival in India makes us as slippery as eels. We are quick to shed our high caste status in the pursuit of a university seat and you'll be surprised how many of these reserved seats end up warmed by privileged bottoms. The most lucrative portfolio to hold, at least down in Tamil Nadu, is Minister of Education. You virtually drown in money helping a child to get a good university education.

'Some students in Hyderabad have sued the university,' Nalini says. 'They're going to prove they passed, but the university gave their marks to another student. And the university failed them.' She pauses in rage. 'God, you don't know what worries we parents have over our children.'

This reality of India makes me even more melancholy than the ruins of Ranthambore. The past is gone and we have already destroyed our future. Govardhan, and thousands like him, pass too quickly from innocence to bitter cynicism. They learn the corroding value of money, the value of influence even as they learn to read and write. And give up hope, for they know intelligence alone will not win them a niche in modern India.

Ratlam

When an English officer disembarked off those gleaming white P&O steamers in Bombay, he made a short tonga ride across the city to Victoria Terminal. There in the cavernous railway station, he would find his reserved compartment on the waiting Frontier Mail. It made a great triangular-shaped run over the face of India, north-east across the Western Ghats, the Deccan and a stopover in Delhi, before turning west once more and chuffing up through Amritsar and finally ending its journey in Peshawar, the gateway to the North-West Frontier. Peshawar now is another country, so my Frontier Mail begins its truncated return haul back to Bombay in Amritsar. But it's running an hour late. Our connecting train in Ratlam is due to leave at 10 p.m. for Indore and we have, unless the Frontier Mail makes up for lost time, missed it already. On the opposite platform, waiting to catch the Frontier Mail heading north to Delhi, I see Tejbir Singh. The rain and the impassable roads have dampened his film-making enthusiasm and I cross the tracks to spend some of my waiting time with him.

We Indians cannot help but ask and answer family questions. His grandfather was knighted by the British for his services as chief contractor for the building of New

Delhi. Tejbir's family still owns a good-sized piece of the city and hence the casual approach to film-making. He studied international politics in the United States and married his childhood sweetheart, Mala. She is the editor of *India* magazine, a good monthly on Indian culture and history. Tejbir and Valmik have also made an award-winning documentary on the ruined Chittor fort and were the liaison for the filming of *The Raj Quartet* television series.

In turn now, he is curious about this journey and its grave-side end in Burhanpur.

'But how can you re-create someone like her?'

'By taking her bits and pieces, and gluing her back together with my imagination. Arjumand must have had some very special quality to have attracted Shah Jahan. There were literally thousands of women in that court, and he could have had any one of them.'

'He fell in love,' Tejbir murmurs practically and with experience in this matter.

Why her? Why not another?

'I'm sure he had an instant erection the moment he saw her in the Royal Meena bazaar, so there was a sexuality in her that out-blazed other women. I wrote of this lust a man has for a woman. But lust is over in a quick burst, so she had to have other qualities. She was a gutsy girl.'

'That's guesswork.'

'No, detective work. You put together the pieces and you have to draw a conclusion. She had the guts to wait for him for five years, the guts to travel all over India with him on his campaigns, the guts to stick by him when things went bad for him.'

'So? Indian women do that even today. It is their dharma.'

'Less and less. As they become economically independent, the chains of duty to a husband weaken. But with Arjumand, the attraction was not the sense of wifely duty, but her power to hold the interest of Shah Jahan. He never re-married when she died. It was a once in a lifetime love. But he did sate his lust on the women around him. While she lived, he never wavered in his love or his lust. There had to be something strong in her to grip the attention of an imperial prince. Wives and women were a dime a dozen in their time.'

Our respective Frontier Mails slide into their platforms, interrupting conversations, but not my train of thought. The ticket collector assigns us our compartment, vaguely promising punctuality in reaching Ratlam. He consoles me with the possibility that my connection too may start off late and we'll therefore catch it. If we miss it, the alternate is a bus to Indore or a one-night stopover in Ratlam.

'I think you're right,' Maureen comments, 'she must have had some special quality which attracted Shah Jahan and mesmerized him.'

'Love is enough,' Nalini sighs. 'It was their karma and they couldn't escape that. She might have been brave and loyal, but the most important thing was she loved him.'

I always find this notion of love strange in India. Here is my sister, married to a stranger at sixteen in traditional style, sighing romantically about love. It's the theme of our movies, the theme of our pop songs, the theme of poets and novelists. This country is saturated with love, with notions of love, with dreams of love, and yet in the very practice of love we retreat into the arranged marriage. In my travels here, how often I've met 'modern' Indian men and women, with doctorates from Yale or Harvard—zestful, energetic, dreaming of love—but the moment they return to the country, they settle for an arranged marriage. They fly 10,000 miles from the United States of America, spend a week viewing prospective matches, pick their partner and, in a jiffy, they're married and off back again to the land of dreams. In our movies too—Hindi, Tamil, Telugu, Bengali—an unreal vision of love exists and is sopped up by huge audiences. It is a melodramatic love of rejection, suicide, death, heartbreak, beatings and one emerges depressed by the complications of this simple moving spirit within us all. But then of course, I realize we do not understand love at all. We fantasize in theory, but never practise it in our private lives. (Yes, yes, there are some 'love' marriages in India, but they are always treated like some rare phenomenon. An aberration). In even our greatest mythological story, the Ramayana, Sita doesn't accompany Rama into exile because of love. No. She is always held up as the perfect example of wifely duty. She trudged after him into the jungle and suffered privation not out of love, but mere duty. She was his wife and these sacrifices were expected of her. The word 'love' never appears once in the Ramayana. And if you should visit during the marriage season and wander the lyrical paths of Kashmir or other popular honeymoon places, you will observe newlyweds behaving as if they were movie heroes or heroines in capturing their photographic memories of them. They will pose like Rekha and Dev Anand by waterfalls, fancy costumes provided by enterprising photographers, only because they have no other idea of love than the movies. The memories they will preserve are not of themselves as lovers holding hands, but of movie stars in some melodramatic epic on love. Who else can they imitate? Their parents—probably another arranged marriage—are not role models for love but of duty, and 'love' is popularized in our movies as a 20th-century invention.

Like our 20th-century train, the great caravan of soldiers and camp followers under the command of Shah Jahan began their fateful journeys south. There were to be many excursions through this landscape of low hills and sparse vegetation.

Shah Jahan's worries are now no greater than mine. Will we make our connection to Indore? The Frontier Mail, instead of making up the time, has begun to lag further. The journey is exhausting for both the train and the passengers, and we settle into the bored attitudes of those crossing an endless Styx. We reach Ratlam finally, way past ten, and a deserted platform. No, not quite. A few people are sitting patiently on their luggage. I race around the platforms looking for a ticket collector, find none and finally stick my head into the station master's office, interrupting a long monologue to a few of his staff, to discover the whereabouts of our connection.

'It hasn't left as yet,' I'm abruptly informed.

I feel some relief. 'When will it leave?'

'When we locate an engine,' he remarks with a resigned air of patience, implying that I should have known this was the reason his train was running a couple of hours late.

'Will that be long?' I enquire politely but receive no reply.

Beyond the iron railings of the station, Ratlam is settling down for the night. A small town with no pretentions to citydom, sighing softly in the last few minutes before sleep. The neon lights flicker like guttering candles, snuffed one by one, and the gentle odour of wood smoke cleans the air.

'Is there anything to see here?' Maureen asks.

'A palace.'

'Why don't we go and have a look then?'

'And miss our train when the stationmaster conjures up an engine?' I'm not feeling adventurous and neither, really, are they. We make ourselves as comfortable as possible, staring across at pigs snuffling between the railway lines and fighting with dogs. Ratlam's small palace lies in the centre of the town. The state named after the town is insignificant today but it does have some historical echoes. Ratlam state was a jagir specially created by Shah Jahan and given by him to the son of Karan Singh. Their friendship extended to this grand gesture but Ratan Singh, the new ruler, did not live too long to enjoy his tiny kingdom. He fought on the side of Dara against Aurangzeb and Murad, and died in battle.

At 11.30, my (I cannot help but feel possessive towards a man with such a calm disposition) stationmaster finally finds a steam engine to pull the train to Indore and we tiredly pile into a carriage. Even though Indore is a mere 92 miles, the train won't arrive until six and we once more sleep restlessly, huddled in our coats, and waking at each stop and start. I dream fitfully that India is overpopulated with railway stations too.

I have a letter of introduction from my father to the Maharaja of Indore. He recalled playing cricket with the prince a half century back and I suspect that since those summery days of his youth, the title has moved on down. It was yet another way my father roamed this country, travelling vast distances and meeting all kinds of men through his love for this game. On the way from the railway station to the Suhag hotel, we pass a large and ornate bungalow. It has vague pretentions to being palatial except for the unpalatial garden.

'Do we introduce ourselves? I ask my companions.

'No,' they both reply, tired of princes too. 'Maybe when we come back from Burhanpur.'

And the palace slides by like an island in a gentle river of traffic. The princely line here are the Holkars who've ruled this town and Indore state, now a part of Madhya Pradesh, since 1733. They were close allies of the British and during the 1857 Revolt, they (a fifteen-year-old boy, Tukoji Rao Holkar II, was on the throne) sided with the British against the rebelling soldiers. This place couldn't have been more than a village on the banks of the river Saraswati in the days of Arjumand.

The hotel Suhag is a five-storey building in subdued iced-cake architecture. It looks a pleasant enough place to rest briefly and bathe after our night of travel, but the receptionist is strangely agitated. She appears in two minds whether to give us rooms or not, hurries away to consult someone and returns to hand us our keys. It is odd, but at this moment, not too disturbing behaviour. But how are we weary travellers to know that karma has a trick still up its sleeve to play on us? But that is to be much later when we are even more unsuspecting.

Burhanpur is now within reach, a mere inch or two on the large map of Madhya Pradesh behind the tourist counter. But I don't want to zip over there directly as Arjumand would not have moved down so swiftly. She would have rested a while in Mandu and then stopped in Asirgarh. The only convenient way from Indore to all these places is by car, and we have an Ambassador and a driver pick us up after lunch. Once we've disposed of our laundry to room service maids, a simple act which is later to involve complications, we take autos into the town. The heart of Indore is the chowk and the old palace.

'There must be loads of antiques here,' Nalini whispers with insatiable greed. 'There aren't any tourists around at all.'

Why she believes she is the first in the chowk to have discovered the value of our old artefacts springs doubtless from eternal optimism. If she had been a Timur, she would have been preoccupied with evaluating and hoarding her plunder. Most of the buildings in the chowk are wooden structures of two floors. The work is simple and undecorative, and after an hour of exploring and harrying the inhabitants for her antiques, we return to the hotel.

'Nothing. Not a thing. Useless people.'

'Well, central India was never famous for any artwork, apart from weaving. The great artisans of the past all worked up north or down south for the princes.'

'They must have made something. Even a teeny weeny bit of old brass would keep me happy.' An antique junkie, unable to get her fix. After lunch, leaving our luggage in the hotel rooms and our keys hanging safely behind the reception counter, we climb into the car for the final leg of our journey. The driver, Ravi, is a thin, small man, almost boy-like, in an immaculately pressed bush shirt and cream slacks. He assures me he knows his Madhya Pradesh like the back of his hand, and we shoot out of the hotel like an arrow. He drives in the normal maniacal style and we calm him down, promising him largesse if he gets us there and back safely.

Ramparts and Ramifications

Indore falls away quickly and the thin black road winds through flat, gently undulating land. The heat should be fierce and unbearable by this time of the year in central India, but the storm that hit us in Ranthambore appears to be following us down south. The sky is darkening, and the small villages and rice fields, separated by great tracts of inhospitable earth, look mellow in the shaded light. Little can grow here in such hard, unyielding soil except scrub and yet, this was all once jungle.

Jahangir complains in his *Jahangir-nama* that on one of his trips down to Mandu a lion attacked his train and killed a pack pony. Deforestation has left not a blade of grass as cover for the poor beast today. The lion which roamed all over central and west India has now retreated to the tiny reserve of Gir, his last and final refuge.

'Where are we going to stay in Mandu?' Nalini suddenly breaks our silence. 'It's all ruin.'

'Ahh, leave it all to me. The archaeological department have a guest house overlooking a tank. It's going to be a fabulous place.'

'What if the guest house is full?' Maureen enquires, knowing how these little inconveniences can occur. 'Government servants have priority.'

'There won't be any there. It's too remote.'

I'm not totally confident, but the location did capture my imagination. I saw it in a photograph. A splendid pink building on the edge of a lotus-filled tank. It looked a seductive, cool place, a restored palace, and it appealed to my sense of imperial imitation. We lapse back into our silences. The land offers us no speculation, just a feeling of sadness. If it were a kinder place, gentler, like those undulating hills of England or those flat pancakes of Kansas, how much richer my country could be. In the distance we glimpse the first outlines, hazy and dreamlike, of the Vindhya mountain chain that divides north India from south. It was those jagged crests of earth that prevented the Muslim invaders from penetrating the south for centuries. But nearer now, rearing straight up from the Narmada plain over which we race, we see the battlements of Mandu. In ancient India, and the ancient world, every town hovered high above the earth like sadhus levitating. It gave them at least a false sense of security. Modern weaponry does not even grant us this comforting illusion.

The car begins its first gear climb up the steep, winding road to the city gates. We pass a villager trudging up, here and there, but not another vehicle. The road winds over a gorge and we peer down on a drop of four or five hundred feet, the sides are sheer as a mountain side. The gorge was a natural moat in this geological formation, isolating a part of the mountain from the rest of the surroundings. The walls of Mandu have long been breached by conquerors and they peter tiredly away around the rim of the hill. Only the monumental Delhi Darwaza and turret remain intact. We pass under the pink sandstone archway decorated in deep blue enamelled mosaic, the ancient wooden gates rotting on giant hinges, and wind down a narrow, dusty road, through a small village nestled outside the ruins. These are the inheritors of Mandu, also known as Shadiabad, or the City of Joy. Beyond the village lie the ruins of Baz Bahadur's palaces. In the twilight, they throw long, sad shadows and when we climb out of the car, the silence is full of ache and memories. The tank which I'd seen in a photograph is a fever of green lotuses and the only preserved building on its north side is built in a tier of rooms and balconies overlooking the water. Ahh, this is what I wanted, and found. I imagine ourselves ensconced in those rooms sitting on the balcony and listening to the ghostly music and laughter.

Nalini reads my mind. She shudders. 'It will be haunted,' she pronounces dramatically and this makes even Maureen pause. 'We'll hear the songs of Rupmati and the sounds of Akbar moving through the grounds. Their spirits are here. I can feel them.'

'Nonsense,' I say firmly but I cannot shake off my deep Indian superstitions of spirits and ghosts, demons and gods returning to earth. 'Those rooms will be perfect.'

The women reluctantly follow me up the steps. A chowkidar sits in a cane chair, already dozing and comes reluctantly awake. The ground floor is a chamber of good size and a dozen carved pillars hold up the roof. In the corner is a dusty glass case containing faded sepia picture postcards of Mandu. It looks as if it has never been opened.

'Do you have vacant rooms?' I ask.

'Yes,' he calls out to someone and a young man ambles

from round the corner. He ducks into a room and brings out a bunch of keys.

'You're going to love this place,' I tell Nalini and Maureen, as we tread the dusty steps up to the next level and the open balcony. Their silence is deafening. It has begun to drizzle but it can't dampen my enthusiasm either. Nothing here appears changed, the India of my childhood returns. Coming up at night to a dak bungalow tucked in a deep recess of India, and finding sparse rooms, lanterns and that immense sense of Indian solitude. 'There's even electricity,' I try to cheer them up.

'Power cut,' the youth says stoically. 'A long time now.'

It is apparently a permanent state of affairs and will last longer as Mandu is high and remote from the rest of India. The rooms are set back from the balcony rails and he opens the first one. In the gloom, filled with the odour of disuse, dust and mouse droppings, we see two neatly made single beds. A table stands between them with a lamp and to a side a comfortable armchair. There is even a glazed porcelain basin and a pitcher, evoking old memories of those days when running water was a luxury. The women hesitantly enter. Beyond the room is another and we peer into an expanse of bathroom with one of the biggest bath tubs I've ever seen. It must be twelve feet long and four wide.

'Looks fine,' I pronounce.

'No, it isn't,' Maureen says.

Nalini merely sniffs and peers nervously around before we examine her room. It is almost identical.

'I don't mind,' Nalini says. 'It reminds me a teeny bit of Hosur, but I don't want any ghosts waking me up.'

'I'm not worried by ghosts,' Maureen states firmly, 'but there are little furry things running around. I saw one disappearing in the other room.'

'I thought I saw something too,' Nalini says with fervour and in no time a shadow has taken on the proportions of a bandicoot or something worse.

'But where else can we stay?'

'There is an Ashoka hotel, sir,' the youth says, relieved for he would have to cook dinner, serve, and fetch and carry. 'It's just further along the road.'

Before he can complete directions, Nalini and Maureen are back in the car. I reluctantly bow to their needs. The ghostly princes and their ladies will have to wait for other guests.

The Ashoka, yet another of the government chain where we raged in Delhi, is a low-lying building well within Mandu and distant from my ruins. It looks deserted but after honking awhile, a fat bearer emerges from a long hibernation to usher us in. In lamp light now, we fill in the register and he leads us to our rooms in a separate section of the building. They are neat, clean and unhaunted, and satisfy the women. When I step out on the rear balcony I see the building stands on the very edge of the crown and the view of the Narmada plain stretches out forever and ever. It's breathtaking, with not a sign of man anywhere and in the distance, like a squiggle on a map, the Narmada river. The silence here is vast with only the wind ruffling the trees and bushes, sighing through the ravine below us. The earth is of an even dun under the cathedral of grey sky and I recall a moment when, somewhere in England, I was taken to a hill and proudly pointed out six counties. Here I cannot see to the edge of the plain.

'In Australia,' Maureen counters, 'you'd only see one ranch.'

Before it gets too dark and the ghost of Baz Bahadur should rise, we stroll down the dirt road to the ruins. We pass through the small village—the tea shop and the provisions store. The only tiny bit of commerce here is glowing with high pressure lantern light and curious children who find not merely Maureen but even Nalini and I exotic. It's too late to thoroughly explore the buildings but in this gloom they appear whole again. In the faint light, the Jahaz Mahal, a pink sandstone roofless palace with the walls curved to resemble the sides of an ancient sea vessel, sails in the ripples of the water on either side. Once upon a time, it was solely occupied by women. And the Hindola Mahal, resembling a palanquin, bows and sways opposite.

'Who was Baz Bahadur?' Maureen asks.

'A sultan of Mandu,' Nalini explains. 'He fell in love with a shepherdess, Rupmati, and married her.' Nalini cannot help but sigh over the love of a king for a singing girl. 'We still sing her songs, you know, they have never been forgotten. Just imagine, she walked along this same path and sat too where we are sitting now looking at the reflections in the lake.'

'What happened to her?'

'She committed suicide.'

'Every woman you talk about committed suicide,' Maureen comments with some asperity. 'Didn't anyone live to a ripe old age and die peacefully? Padmini, now Rupmati.'

'If you were beautiful then,' I hasten to explain these

dramatic deaths, 'you committed suicide only because you were lusted after by some conqueror or the other.'

'Death rather than defilement,' Nalini announces to the still waters of the tank. 'They were Hindu women, the conquerors were Muslim.'

How would an unconquered people like the Australians understand the horrors of plunder, rape, the sword? They are deeply ingrained in our psyche, in our Hindu mythology. Sita was captured by the demon king Ravana and because she was suspected of having been defiled by Ravana during her captivity, the heroic Rama rejected her in spite of her protestations of purity. Here in Mandu, Rupmati became the object of desire of Akbar's General, Adham Khan, in 1562. Akbar sent Adham Khan to capture Mandu and Baz Bahadur fell in the last pitched battle under the Delhi Darwaza. Adham Khan then marched to the harem and demanded Rupmati. Legend has it she sent him sweetmeats and wine and sang her famous songs to him from behind the jali of the harem. Then she appeared in all her silks and finery and fell dead at his feet. Adham Khan discovered she had hidden poison in her hathphool (an elaborate hand ornament of rings and flowers) and in a rage, threw the other women in the harem to his troops and set fire to Mandu. He plundered the treasury and sent a token of it, and a few women, to Akbar, but on his return to Agra he paid the ultimate price for these acts. Akbar had him thrown off the walls of the fort, and when he didn't die the first time, Adham Khan was dragged up and hurled down once more. I suspect he was killed more for his sleight-of-hand with the plunder than his destruction of Mandu. Many years later, Akbar finally visited Mandu. Adham Khan had left a ghostly ruin and Akbar, to make amends, restored the palaces, repaired the tanks and built a spacious palace for himself, the Nilkanth Mahal which overlooks the Narmada valley. This was one of the rare places where Akbar enjoyed peace and quiet in his hectic life. From then on, Mandu became another Mughal motel. Jahangir, Shah Jahan and Aurangzeb would rest here before continuing south to the battlefields of the Deccan. Arjumand bore two of her children here, Roshanara and Murad.

The chilly wind has picked up strength, ruffling the waters, sighing through the skeletons of the palaces and I can see Nalini's anxiety. If we listen carefully, we can hear the whispers of Rupmati's melodious voice, the rage of Adham Khan, the footsteps of Akbar, Arjumand's voice calling her children, the chink-chink of the harem women as they gathered around the water in the late evening to listen to music and feast and dance. A drizzle, fine as mist, veils the ruins and we reluctantly leave them to the gathering darkness.

As we walk through the village and the pin-points of yellow lamplight, poor people huddled in the shadow of ghostly splendour, I recall the lines of the English historian Mountstuart Elphinstone. In his *History of India* (1841), he wrote: 'Those who look on India in its present state may be inclined to suspect the native writers of exaggerating its former prosperity; but the deserted cities, ruined palaces and choked-up aqueducts which we will see, with the great reservoirs and embankments in the midst of jungles, and the decayed causeways, wells, and caravanserais of the royal roads, concur with the evidence of contemporary travellers in convincing us that those historians had good grounds for their commendation.'

The small empty hotel is a depressing place. Modern India ground to discomfort by the power cut and we search for the bearer. We find him in the kitchen, sitting alone in the dim lamplight. He stirs himself to bring us hot water for our baths and we order dinner from a grubby, plastic-protected menu. It is best in the remote fastnesses of India to order simple foods: rice, dals, vegetables, dahi, but in a flush of hunger we ask for chicken curry. He promises to make us an excellent one. After our buckets of hot water, we sit beside the window looking out on the rain coming down in flashing curtains. The plain far below is momentarily lit, impressed on our collective retinas as a surrealistic landscape of emptiness, and then returns to the blackness.

Suddenly, harshly, our electric lights spring on and the fan stirs lazily overhead. It is an odd time for power to be restored and it flickers hesitantly, trying to make up its mind and then remains. Our dinner across in the empty dining room on formica tables is adequate, though the chicken was without doubt the scrawniest that lived. And with even less doubt, the most expensive. The bearer presents the bill. One chicken: rupees hundred (circa 1983).

'One hundred rupees for a chicken curry? Badmash, who do you think we are.'

He looks at us sullenly. 'You asked for four dishes of chicken ... see.' He whips out the menu. 'One chicken dish is 25 rupees. You had four dishes. One hundred rupees.'

'I don't believe it,' Nalini explodes. 'You don't pay that much for chicken in Delhi or Bombay.'

'One hundred rupees,' he intones and there is no bargaining, no budging the man in his demands. He waves the menu around in our faces like a fan to douse our passion.

We pay, grumbling away to ourselves, knowing full well we've been taken for a classic ride. A chicken in the bazaar, live and whole, would cost a quarter that amount, less even, as Nalini assures me, and here in Mandu not even five rupees. I suspect the bearer has a chicken ranch as valuable as minks in the hotel backyard.

I rise a half hour before the sun. In that primeval darkness India looks new. The earth, brushed by the pale pink sky, looks virginal, vigorous and abundant. The illusion swiftly vanishes as the sun breaks above the horizon, golden and harsh, revealing the endless plain to be brown and hard and sterile. What has changed since Baz Bahadur and Rupmati, Shah Jahan and Arjumand, eternal lovers, gazed down from where I stand? Not the mountains, not the sky, only the earth. It has been sucked dry over three centuries, vanquished so easily by man. It could not cry for help, secretly knowing that its vengeance would descend on the future. On the children and their children and their children's children. The earth has a truly primeval concept of vengeance; it awaits our descendants to launch its savage assault. There is never any forgiveness unless we offer it the homage of care, water, tending, love.

After a cautious prix fixe breakfast, we walk over to the Jami Masjid which is on the opposite side of the village from the palaces. The massive mosque is built as an open square, surrounded by a multi-arched wall with each arch capped with a small dome. The main prayer hall itself is topped with two large domes, dark and mossed with the years but the finial still glows golden and burnished. Within, the walls are crowded with carvings and on one side stairs lead up to a stone canopy. It was built in 1454 and in spite of the passage of 530 years and neglect, it looks as new as yesterday. A few children gather around us as we wander into the cool interior. Bats clings to the ceiling and the air is stale with their odour. Maureen and Nalini eye them nervously as we caress the granite walls and the finely carved pillars. Islam could not escape the influence here of the Hindu artisans. It has obviously not been used for worship for countless years, although experts believe this is the finest piece of Afghan architecture in India. It is also supposedly the biggest mosque in Asia but its emptiness resounds like a kettle drum.

In the next compound is the exquisite marble tomb of the builder Alif Khan Hoshang Shah Ghori(1406–35). It is quite impossible to describe the emptiness of this frozen splendour, so far from the eyes of man. From the air, I'm told, you can look down on its beautiful white dome and believe it to be the Taj Mahal. The resemblance is not surprising as Shah Jahan is said to have sent his architects down here to study the building. Only a few villagers now pursue their goats along the pathways cut in the hard, dry earth on their way to the grazing grounds. They give these buildings barely a glance, it's just part of their landscape.

With the sun high and hard, the puddles of the night's rain shrivel and vanish even as we watch them. The air is humid as we return to the palaces. Their reflections in the water are still and sharp, framed against the brassy blue sky.

We wander through ruins, pillars standing alone and forlorn and hamams, beautifully proportioned, now filled with dust and dirt. They look like the forerunners to jacuzzis with openings in all sides of the human-height tub. It could have been a marvellous place for orgies. But it's all silent now, only the gentle hum of insects, and quite, quite forgotten. The lust and passion has faded into the wavering air of history.

But Baz Bahadur built a separate palace for himself and his singer. It is at the far end of the table of Mandu and we drive across flat barren land. It once contained a city, but from the nakedness of the earth—here and there are weak efforts of cultivation but mostly, the land looks iron-hard—who would believe this once teemed with life, bazaars, streets, and citizens? How swiftly ordinary people disappear from the earth while the monuments of kings remain as empty reminders of forgotten glories. Those Indian towns and villages would have been built out of mere mud, and when the princes fell they dissolved back to the dust from which they had risen. In the *Ain-i-Akbari*, Abul Fazal complains about the ability of the Indian village to appear and disappear almost overnight, and the major problem of the Mughals was, because of the emptiness of the land, to keep the villagers pinned down to one place and cultivate crops. Mandu was once, at its height, 20 square miles in area.

Rupmati's palace, in those days, must have stood at the far end of town, a choice piece of ancient suburbia. Now her ruined palace looks out on the most spectacular view of the Narmada valley. It is a desolate building, choked with earth and weeds, and we have to clamber over a wall to stand on the palace floor. The only piece of architecture not to have fallen completely is a red sandstone pavilion. It is rectangular and domed and stands at the very edge, looking out across the plains. Here, I imagine, Baz Bahadur and Rupmati spent the twilights gazing upon each other and India. No doubt, Arjumand and Shah Jahan too occupied this palace. Apart from this graceful pavilion nothing else remains, except the sky above and broken pillars and archways forming the four sides of the palace. Bush and grass have reclaimed the earth from her grandeur.

We clamber down, unable to grasp even the slightest sense of the tragic heroine. A dirt road leads north, sloping downwards, and we follow it until we come to a small temple, built into the side of the cliff. It hangs about 30 feet below the level of Mandu and is shaded by two great bodhi trees. The steps down are sharp and steep, and it is a relief to escape the sun. In the pleasantly cool shade, a priest sits on the steps. The temple is flat-roofed, with steps leading up to the sanctum, and facing a small courtyard. Just beneath the steps is a beautiful little fountain. It looks an illusion, carved from granite. It's about ten feet square but within the square is carved a sinuous maze of curves. The water rises from beneath the steps, flows through the intricate pattern and down into a tank. The water looks clear and cool and deceptively still.

Nalini cannot resist puja and we clamber up the steps. The priest, a middle-aged man, accepts our coins and murmurs a prayer before the ancient idol of Shiva. He is unadorned, not dazzling us worshippers with silks and diamonds and gold tiaras, as once he had to for these ancient ghosts. Now, only the poor offer their flowers and meagre coins.

'Maybe,' Nalini whispers, hands clasped, head bowed, 'Rupmati too prayed here.' She is determined to preserve this shadowy woman who by suicide chipped a niche for herself in our historical imaginations.

'Ask the priest how old the temple is?'

He replies merely, 'Old, very old.' And ends there, unable to stretch out the length of time, like chewing gum, to some finite starting point.

Perhaps Rupmati stood here then, and also Aurangzeb, the Shadow of Allah, the Seizer of the Universe. He checked his hand, nothing here is worth the effort of his destruction. Mandu now has exhausted our curiosity. We look out at the glaring emptiness of the plain below, the land around. Goats and cattle, followed by little boys and girls, nibble scrub for survival.

Our car sweeps by the ruins and our last glimpse is of desertion and then I have the driver pause a moment, teetering on descent, beneath the Delhi Darwaza. Delhi, far, far to the north, beyond the horizon, and yet imprinting its name on this entrance. Then we sweep down to the plain and are immersed in the heat and dust of India. It hasn't rained down here for... centuries, it seems. The earth is brittle as paper, with dry, swirling dust. Every ten minutes or so, the wind, like a man twirling candy floss, spins a cone of dust out of the land, tosses it up high into a funnel and races over the empty landscape, turning the sky brown with dust and dead leaves, before allowing it to collapse back into the earth. Only to begin again, as if trying to free itself from the chains of this dreadful destiny. The tarmac road shimmers ahead, wavering in that terrible heat, also wishing to dissolve before we can race over it. It undulates through gentle hills and valleys, which should evoke in your minds green and soothing pastures. Instead, stunted trees, leafless, cling to the earth by roots like the claws of a skeleton reaching out from a grave. It seems the trees are topsy-turvy and are holding on grimly, for otherwise they would fly away.

A tribal family shelters under a thatch awning, castaways in a cruel island of shade. As if we do not have the complexities of castes and religions, we have too our tribals and aborigines, our Mayans and our Maoris. I was informed once by an elegant government lady that the problem was that 'India is on the fast track and we're trying not to destroy the tribals on the slow one,' and I could not help but wonder how American terminology could apply to this ancient country, these pre-Hindu people. Did they, when she descended on them from Delhi, understand their problem in terms of tracks, or, like me, look bewildered.

There are many tribals in India, tucked away in the jungles and ravines, in remote fastnesses of mountains and desiccated deserts, disappearing and yet being revealed bit by bit. The Nagas and the Adivasis, the Todas and the gypsies, living simple and spartan lives on roots and rabbits. They are our true ancestors, for once we too were tribals, and not as now, ancestral villagers. With Darwinian evolution, we escaped the jungles and carried away those ancient habits of worship of things primeval and natural. Hinduism, the philosophy, is but the veneer covering these ancient Vedic beliefs: in the power of Agni our fire god, Vanaspati, the Lord of the Forests, Garuda the eagle, Surya the sun, Vayu the wind. In their lost hopelessness, unable to comprehend the technological forces which now sweep the surface of our thoughts, the tribals still worship those ancient gods, praying no doubt not to be run down by the India on her fast track. But they have little chance, like the jack rabbits and foxes on the super highways of America, they will soon be flattened and flung aside.

Their lands have already been eroded, their women used and abused by officials and contractors and landlords eager for the rape of both property and flesh. Little remains except the indignity of integration, the indignity of reservations or else a miserable death.

My father once knew this part of India well. He came often, clutching blueprints of dreams to transform the lives of these sad and sorry people. The mainspring in my father's heart, the pumping blood of his daily life, was to change India.

'What happened to his scheme?' Nalini asks me softly as we leave our tribals behind, watching the automobile rushing us over this nightmarish land.

'What scheme?' Maureen asks, the stranger unaware of family secrets, forgotten now in our crowded memories.

'Well,' I cannot but hesitate, as even my memory has clouded over its details, but there still remained a nobility of purpose in his idea that made me not ashamed. 'He wanted to build a milk powder plant not far from here... a hundred or so miles south in a place called Bastar. The cattle would be provided by international organizations and given to these tribals. So they would have a living. They would be taught and financed to stall-feed their cows, and the milk would be collected daily for the plant.' I have of course reduced years of his life and thoughts to a few seconds of words.

'What happened?' is her necessary question, for those plans now gather the eternal Indian dust.

'It failed because he did not have the necessary commercial greed.' I cannot disguise my bitterness again. 'It failed because he could not bribe the right government officials. It failed because there was no profit for anyone except the tribals ... and who cares about them.'

'He always had such great ideas,' Nalini comments sadly and we lapse into separate silences.

He is not a political man, yet in his own way he too wanted India to change, to race into the 20th century on the fast track. But with a care for those things in India he loves passionately. From his student days in the early 1920s, after Oxford, when he turned down a job offer in England to return to India because he felt his talents were more necessary here than there, how we have, as a people, swelled the coffers of other nations with our brains and our brawn.

It's a 90-minute drive to Maheshwar, the old capital of Indore state, on the banks of the Narmada. It's a small, quiet town, dozing a long dream. We pull up at a miniature (if we are to measure this place against the grandeur of a Mandu or a Jaipur) fort. It really is a simple place, more a home for a well-to-do landlord than the residence of the Holkar princes. It's a traditional square with the rooms facing into the courtyard. The rooms are roped off and contain simple, if antique (and my sister drools enviously) furniture. A few glass cabinets contain smaller artefacts. But it's when we wander down a corridor, out into the sunlight and turn a corner that we come upon sudden splendour. Silver chairs and cradles, beyond iron bars, and chowkidars on guard. There is another, homely, touch—countless sepia photographs of the Holkar family and, for some strange reason, the princes appear to be called by common Christian names, Fred and John and Harry, and the women resemble American heiresses.

The land slopes down from this mansion and we can just catch a glimpse of a temple, enough for Nalini to pursue. The road is dusty, narrow and deserted, with the temple wall to the right of us, and to the left a row of buildings with signs hung above the doors: Cooperative this and Cooperative that. Maureen disappears into the first door, while Nalini and I continue down. It's a beautiful old temple, serene in its emptiness, calm in its neat cleanliness. A priest sits with his back to one of the sculpted pillars and watches us move around, exclaiming at this carving or that.

'Where are you from?' he suddenly asks in perfect English.

'South India.'

'Ahh, you have more beautiful temples there.' He heaves himself up. A portly man, bare chested, with a calm and pleasant face. He gives us a guided tour of the temple, pointing to the myriad gods and goddesses wrought in stone on the ceilings and the walls. He draws us naturally towards the sanctum and the black stone idol, garlanded with fresh flowers, draped in silks and glittering diamonds and gold, such a distance between this one and the poor fellow in Mandu. The priest rings the bell to awaken God for our prayers, lights camphor, accepts our coins and intones a shloka. His arti is done swiftly and then he graciously retires back to his resting place. The temple remains deserted, but it rambles along, like a miniature self-contained town. So many carvings, worn smooth by the countless years, animals and gods, gambolling in tiers, higher and higher. The granite beneath our bare feet sears the soles and we hop around swiftly, grateful for the shade.

'Where's Maureen?' Nalini suddenly asks.

'How do I know? She went into some building.'

'How can you just do that to her? She could be lost.' Nalini panics, feeling I have cruelly abandoned my wife.

'You don't know her.'

'This is India, not England or America. Anything can happen.'

She is not to be placated and we hurry out of the temple to comb the warren of small houses alongside the temple. It isn't bustling with life, in fact from the exterior, it is somnambulant in the afternoon sun. We pop our heads into the building we'd seen her enter and she is still there, quietly watching the women at work. Nalini and I love the house, the inward square, full of calm and light and greenery. The women work at ancient looms, making bedcovers and tablecloths, shirts and napkins. In charge of around twenty women, is a sole young man sitting at a desk with papers in front of him and behind are neatly packed bales of these products destined to end up in the far corners of India and the world to fetch exorbitant prices. The women are delighted with Maureen's interest and attention, and chatter and giggle to each other and her. A baby holds our attention, gripping Maureen's fingers and staring with open-mouthed curiosity at her yellow hair.

'We have to buy some things,' Maureen says. 'But will

these women get any of it or does it just go into someone else's pocket?'

I repeat her question to the youth who looks at us with dismay. 'Sir, this is a cooperative. These women will get equal benefit from whatever we sell.' He shuffles through papers, pulls more out of drawers. 'See, these are our rules and regulations. We cannot cheat them.'

Sighing, I accept his protestation though I visualize the escalation in prices, rippling ever outward from here. Middlemen multiplying and fattening on the talented labour of these women. We buy whatever we can. Shirts, bedspreads, tablecloths, our conscience sopped temporarily by our paltry munificence. Yet what else can we give. Empty compassion or the sinew of their needs—money. At least here, they can watch the money change hands, see their percentages in cash rather than numbers on a piece of paper flourished under their noses.

Asirgarh

Too swiftly now the car rushes towards Burhanpur along the narrow tarmac ridge threaded through this cruel landscape. I feel dread. It is a place of dying, this Burhanpur, this dot in India. I suddenly feel wearied too, not wanting to complete this journey. There is still time to turn back to Indore and allow Burhanpur to remain mainly a figment of my imagination, a figment of India's memory too, long forgotten on the banks of the Tapti.

'Nonsense,' Nalini says. 'Aren't you curious to see where she lies? I am. I didn't even know she died here.'

So there is no retreat with sister and wife. They are morbidly curious to discover Arjumand's first grave. Is it of marble too, or rich sandstone? Or maybe it doesn't exist at all? Like Mandu, like Ranthambore, like countless other places that once stood so firm on this earth, it could have vanished.

'Graves always remain,' Maureen says. 'They are tended more carefully than the homes of the living. Look at all the graves you see in England, Australia, Europe. We worship the places of our dead. They are places for pilgrimage like this one.'

Death, death, death. It's the rhythm of the searing heat

flowing through the open windows of the car and the hum of its tyres. Even our stomachs seem to growl to this rhythm and we remember we've not eaten all day. A small town looms out of the shimmer of land and scrub, settled across the crossroad which disappears into the brown horizon.

'Where shall we eat?' Nalini peers doubtfully at the dhabas alongside the road.

They are small open rooms, some thatch-roofed, with benches and bare tables, flies, and chhokras swabbing down tables and carrying steaming dishes to hungry men and women. The dekchis on the clay fires bubble and simmer, hygienically destroying the bacteria. We choose one with a small sign of modernity—an ice box behind the cashier. The place, however, is no different. I give tiffin money to the driver and he wanders away to eat by himself and we settle ourselves at the tables with chilled bottles of Limca. Maureen fastidiously tries to clean the table, and Nalini cannot help chuckling. It is like Hercules cleaning the stables. The flies merely buzz and return. The food we order is simple and tasty: channa masala, rice, parathas, dahi, served on leaves. There is no meat to be had, meat being the luxury of the rich. And after we have eaten, the Sikh owner of the dhaba allows us to use his private bathroom at the back. We enter a delightful courtyard, filled with plants and a large spacious room and in a small corner room a modern flush toilet. He has hidden away his wife and family behind the facade of a poor dhaba place.

The driver belches contentedly, and we sweep out of the small unremarkable gathering of houses on the road to Burhanpur. The land turns more hilly but doesn't change its drab colouring. Deeper in the hills, as the car cautiously takes the curves and twists, we come upon a strange sight. It's not the overturned lorry, for they are anything but strange on the highways of India, but its cargo. It's a massive piece of 20th-century technology: a sort of pipe, intricately made, something nuclear in its sheen and the metallic bits and pieces attached. It lays, slain here, in the middle of nowhere. It has been here some time, the driver of the lorry has made himself a makeshift shelter and has his pots and pans laid out neatly. He lies in that shade watching us, waiting, waiting, for rescue. He can be rescued, but who is going to rescue this massive piece of technology? How can it be lifted back onto the lorry? Where will it be going? Where did it come from? Where does it fit in our dreams of the future? Somewhere beyond these hills men and machines await this giant jigsaw, brooding on how to load it back onto the lorry. It fades from view but not from memory. It worries and puzzles me even now as I write about it. They will need a giant crane to lift it but there are no cranes within a hundred miles, I suspect. So it will have to trundle in from Indore or Bhopal, taking weeks to crawl these roads to resuscitate this dinosaur lying on the road.

'Look ... look,' Maureen says suddenly as the car turns a curve and straight ahead, rearing out of the land, we see the chilling black fortress of Asirgarh. It looks a fearsome place with its blackened sides, a place of rakshasas and dark magic, brooding high, high above the land. It is the highest fort in India and rears a sheer 1,000 feet straight up. The hill on which it stands is virtually perpendicular and stripped of all cover, but there is an ancient dirt road creeping and clinging to its side like the coils of an emaciated snake.

'Can we go up?' I ask the driver.

He nods cheerfully, stops at the bottom and changes down to first gear. The road is so steep he never has to change gears and we creep up and up, the land falling away, the wheels on the very edges of the dirt, sending gravel bouncing and skittering down. The scrub here is standing out vertically like the hairs on a frightened man's nape. Only betrayal could have ever conquered this place.

And it was through betrayal that Akbar captured this iron fortress. It has a dim and opaque history as do all old things in India. Legend, our convenient amnesia, has it that this fort was built by Ashwatthama, one of the heroes of the *Mahabharata*. It is said that after he participated in the Mahabharata war, he went into voluntary exile which brought him to this wild and desolate place. The fort does, as we circle nearer, look that old. The granite blocks of the walls are black with age and weather; the men who built this, built it to survive until the end of the earth itself. It looks a part of the earth, a part of its very beginning, a part of the boulders and rocks below the walls. There is no beauty except the beauty of sheer power and even though long-deserted, you can feel the vibrations of its arrogance. It frightens. The car stops finally, and we can look far down to the plain and crane our necks to stare up at the vertical walls. They tower a couple of hundred feet still higher. No medieval army had a hope of breaching these walls or scaling them or bombarding them. A stairway, four horsemen wide, curves up alongside the walls always within view of the battlements. The silence of this place is broken only by the sigh of the breeze and the sad keening cries of circling kites.

A familiar blue metal plaque set into the wall reduces all its centuries of existence down to a few lines.

'This is one of the highest hill forts of India with abundant supply of water in its tanks and commands all roads from north India. It is attributed to the epic hero Asvathama. Traditions speak of its being ruled by a herdsman, Asa Ahir. The fort consists of three lines of defense of which the uppermost is known as Asirgarh proper. The middle one as Kamargarh and the lower one as Malaigarh. The main entrance to the fort on the south-east passes through the five gateways by a steep ascent of steps. Asirgarh was ruled by the Chauhan Rajputs till AD 1295 when Alauddin Khilji stormed it and put its garrison to the sword. Subsequently it was occupied by the Faruqui kings of the Khandesh from about AD 1400 to 1600 and was strengthened by them. The lower part Malaigarh has been constructed by Adil Khan I (1438–41). The Faruquis took refuge at Asirgarh whenever their capital Burhanpur was threatened by invaders. In AD 1600 the Mughal emperor Akbar (1556–1605) annexed Khandesh and captured Asirgarh along with defender Bahadur Khan, the last Faruqui king, after a protracted siege. A contemporary inscription cut in the rock near the main gateway of Asirgarh records this event. The fort was captured by the Peshwa Balaji Rao II (1749–61) in AD 1760 and passed from the Scindias to the hands of the British in AD 1819. (Archaeological Survey of India).'

We begin the climb in uneasy silence. The granite steps have been worn down by the trampling of countless armies and it's truly a place I would not wish to spend the night in.

'What happens if it's locked?' Nalini whispers and it's a place for whispers and secrets already.

'We'll see. Save your breath. It's a long climb.'

The plaque is too kind to the conquerors of this place. Each time it fell, it was a man within betraying his comrades. Akbar besieged it for a full year and knew, as one of the greatest generals who even took Chittor, he could never take this place. He camped in Burhanpur during the siege which was really hopeless. The fort had abundant water (supposedly a secret underground spring) and ample food stocks. He tried bombarding these walls but even a cruise missile would have trouble making a dent, and those ancient cannon balls just bounced off harmlessly. He tried mining the walls but even that had no effect. He even tried the sabat, or covered trench, with which he took Chittor but the ground here is too steep on which to build and if he began on the plain below it would have taken a century for the tunnel to rise to the height of the wall. Finally, frustrated, he turned to cunning. He invited the Faruqui king to a conference below, guaranteeing him safe return, but when the king came, Akbar imprisoned him. The king's son, however, refused to capitulate, distrusting Akbar's word. And then Akbar dangled the ancient carrot—gold, to the men in the fort—and magically the great gates opened and his army poured in. Even Troy could not have been more impregnable than this place.

There are no longer any doors, only the massive gateways, each one defendable, the granite blocks unscarred by war. We climb and climb, under archways, passing under the five gates, until we finally come out in the open and desolation. It is surprisingly cool, almost chilly. The area within contains only fallen walls, walkways, graves, ruins, scrub and many trees, and in the far corner the Masjid built by Shah Jahan still dominates. It is surprisingly intact and we start our exploration in that direction.

Quite suddenly, scaring us out of our wits, a man materializes from the shadows. He is ancient, seamed, dark and wears a frayed sort of uniform. He salaams and announces he works for the Archaeological Survey of India and is the chowkidar. He says no more but instead watches us impassively. This is his kingdom now.

And then, as these things are wont to happen in India when you think you have left all signs of men, a young couple materialize from behind another ruined wall. They are neatly, sweetly, dressed: the man in his twenties, with a neat bush shirt, and dhobied trousers, the girl in a brightly coloured saree. Between them is a small tiffin carrier and a basket and we realize they are here on a picnic.

'How did they get up here?' Nalini asks in wonder.

'They walked,' Maureen says. 'There are steps from the very bottom.'

I sense Maureen's unease. Once more, as in Shivpur, she finds herself in the remote strangeness in India. The brooding fort and this young man who watches us in coiled silence. The woman ignores us and begins to spread out her picnic in the shade of a bodhi tree.

'Ignore them,' I tell Maureen but she cannot. It is hard to soothe the fear of a place so strange and far from all her experiences.

Reluctantly, she follows us along the battlements. The plain stretches hazily away into the distance and there, south, glittering silver like a single strand of wire, the Tapti and beside it a small town.

'Burhanpur.' Yet it wavers, receding and approaching, something more imagined than real. When we look directly down we are surprised to find kites circling a hundred feet below us and I'm reminded of the comment by an English writer: 'The natives in their high-flown way, say of this fort that none but the crafty hawk high, lingering over his prey, or the morning lark singing over its young, could ever see in the inside of Aseerghur...' Why, I wonder, could the English never spell our towns correctly?

Nalini has been patrolling a different section of the battlements, over the entrance, and she calls me over urgently. When Maureen and I peer down, we see far below, the driver talking to the young man who moments ago was standing not far from us.

'What are they talking about?' Nalini wants to know.

'They may be plotting something,' Maureen says with a touch of panic. 'Go down and find out.'

'That's a long walk,' I protest.

'Go on,' Nalini orders, also feeling uneasy. 'He may be planning to bump off the driver and then where will we be?'

'I'll drive,' but my crack is ignored and both their faces are stern.

Sighing mightily, I start down and half way I meet the young man running up. He studiously ignores me as we pass and when I reach the car I find the driver stretched out asleep in the back. 'What did he want?' I wake him.

'Where you all are from, Sir. I told him, Indore.' He looks politely enquiring, quite hearty and I leave him to doze.

The trudge back takes twice as long and when I reach the fort, I see no sign of the women at first but only of the young couple settling down to their picnic. It was, I admit, an adventurous act: to have caught a morning bus from whereever, climbed a thousand feet and spread out a lunch in the same spot, more or less, where Akbar, Shah Jahan and Arjumand and Aurangzeb once stood.

I take my own route, catching a quick glimpse of blonde hair and bright saree moving in the distant ruins. The gentle breeze and the circling hawks keep me company as I stroll along the battlements. There is an empty tank (so much for the underground spring) towards the centre of the fort and beside it an English cemetery. I jump over the low granite wall and peer at the headstones; even from a foot away I can read nothing. The stone has been worn down by the wind and rain and the inscriptions are indecipherable. What a strange place in which to die. Thousands of miles from their homeland, a thousand feet above the face of India, suspended between earth and heaven. The forgotten loneliness of this cemetery depresses me. Who pays homage or makes a pilgrimage now to these strangers with erased names and deeds?

I catch up with the women within the ruin of the Masjid. The great dome is intact but the walls sprout weeds and plants and the rubble underfoot makes walking difficult.

It was here, in 1626, that Shah Jahan proclaimed himself Emperor of Hindustan. He knelt in prayer and read from the Quran. Arjumand sat in the women's enclosure and watched him transform from prince to the Padshah Shah Jahan, Sovereign of the World, the Shadow of Allah, the Scourge of God, the Lord of the Rivers and Lord of the Seas, the Administer of Justice, the Conqueror. It was a minute of history, the youth, the descendant of Timur-i-Leng, Babur, Humayun, Akbar and Jahangir, and father of Aurangzeb, taking on the mantle of power. How men here must have performed kornish, bowed, prostrated themselves before the new Great Mughal. Here, here, here… where we stand and leave our dusty footprints on the broken floor of the mosque.

And it was at this same moment that a woman called Arjumand Banu was reincarnated into the Empress Mumtaj-i-Mahal, Exalted One of the Palace. On this woman he loved so much, he bestowed other titles too—Malika-i-Jahan (Queen of the World) and Malika-uz-Zamani (Queen of the Age). Unlike Mehrunissa, she did not usurp Shah Jahan's power when he became Emperor. She supported and advised him and he would send her the state papers to read, approve and stamp with the royal seal that she kept in the harem.

We spend an hour exploring what remains, so little of once such a mighty place. The young couple are stretched out close to each other, dozing on a blanket and the chowkidar asks for a tip which I give him, this guardian of so much history who now holds ghostly armies at bay within his frayed uniform. Is he remembered by those people up in Delhi that he guards the great Asirgarh fortress?

'How long have you worked here?' I ask.

'All my life,' his answer is stoical as if I'd asked a foolish question.

'Do many people visit this place?'

'Very few.' He looks around. 'I am here to protect it from damage. Soon I will be retiring.'

'Do you know everything about this fort?'

'What is everything? Only what is on the plaque.'

It was here in Asirgarh that Shah Jahan received the urgent message from Burhanpur, that his wife, Arjumand, was seriously ill. He rode night and day to cover the 22 kilometres to be by her side as she died.

Burhanpur

It's not far now from here to Arjumand's grave, fifteen minutes by car to cover the 22 kilometres to Burhanpur. We reach as twilight softly starts to creep over the land.

It is 1630 and Arjumand has been Empress for four years. Such a short time. She is no longer the wife of the bi-daulat, no longer travelling as some paltry princess in a carriage but in the meghdabar, a gold and jewelled throne set atop an elephant. She is tired and old beyond her 35 years, exhausted by travel, wearied by the thirteen children that have flowed from her womb. A fourteenth now waits, to spring to life and drag her down to her death.

The baby was born near the lower rim of the empire, a daughter, Gauhar Ara. The landscape, the people, the climate, all were inhospitable. The hills were a dull purple, sharp as teeth, rising above a mass of jungle containing isolated villages and petty princes. Burhanpur was an important city under the Rashtrakuta Dynasty who ruled from 753–982. Malik Nasir Khan of the Faruqi dynasty captured it in 1388, and re-named it after the Sufi saint Burhan-ud-din. Akbar annexed the Khandesh Sultanate in 1601 and made Burhanpur the capital of the Khandesh Subah. He renamed Khandesh after his son Danesh who died of alcoholism when he was thirty-three. But before his death he built the beautiful Shahi Qila. Jahangir appointed his son Parvez as governor in 1609 and Burhanpur flourished as the capital of the Deccan. And when Shah Jahan lived there he added a rooftop garden to the Shahi Qila. In those days there was a constant bustle of boats plying between here and Surat, along the Tapti River. The river lapped the palace walls, and from the parapets, the inhabitants could glimpse through the haze the great brooding rock fortress, Asirgarh. The road runs parallel to the old walls of Burhanpur, plastered now with posters and daubed with slogans. The Qila's battlements are no more than twenty feet high and the gates into the town no longer exist. The walls come to a shattered end, like a frayed nerve, and the town spills out like uncontrollable flesh.

'Do you know where the palace is?' Nalini asks the driver.

'Yes, Memsahib,' he answers confidently and we spend fifteen lost minutes as he inches through the small lanes and alleys of old Burhanpur. The two-storey houses are huddled together like in those old towns of Ajmer and Agra. People have clung to each other for comfort for a thousand years of upheavals and still live according to their ancient ways. Goats and children gambol in the streets and the bazaar sells the mere necessities for men and women.

'There must be some antiques here,' Nalini says hopefully, constantly avaricious for her plunder. 'This place is over a thousand years old.'

'It's all been taken,' I tell her. 'Long before you were born the invaders came.'

Even in such smallness our driver can't find the palace and I finally get him to stop and ask for directions. We have been circling for half an hour and my impatience is unbearable. The directions he receives are simple. A left and a right...

And the ruined Shahi Qila stands before us. Only half of it remains, a few roofless walls silhouetted against the blue sky. By us, where we park, a couple of walls stand apart like forgotten memories. The entrance is a turnstile, and we enter a small garden, the lawn worn in patches like an old carpet. A small fountain stands in the centre with nothing in it. At the far end of the garden stands the 'palace'—a raised chamber, broken-walled, archways overlooking the Tapti.

'How sad,' my sister murmurs. 'Can't these damned archaeological people take better care of this place?'

'You can't teach archaeology to a people who have no concept of history. This is just a ruin... nothing more.'

I climb the few steps and stand... where? It is impossible to tell which part of the palace I'm in—is it the Diwan-i-Khas, the Diwan-i-Aam, the Ghusl khana? To my left is a smaller chamber while to my right the palace ends, but then when I peer over the wall and down to the river, I see more of the palace, a broken limb of it to the far right. Below the limb is a honeycomb of chambers.

'Where is her grave?'

The question lingers in the warm, still air. That is what I have come here for. I look over the fat, placid Tapti, and the land beyond which slopes up gently into fields and trees and then I know intuitively, I am looking at Arjumand's grave. It stands in the fading sunlight just in front of a grove of trees. The tomb is a wall, a dozen feet high, with minarets on either ends and a small arch over the centre. It is of simple red brick, darkened now by centuries. It looks forlorn and lost in the open fields.

'That's it.'

'How do you know?'

'I know. She was first buried on the banks of the Tapti.'

My word is silently accepted. Arjumand's screams linger in memory, dying in childbirth in this forgotten place. And on her death, somewhere here near where we stand, the Great Mughal Shah Jahan began his eight days and nights of mourning. He closed the palace, drove out all courtiers and servants, and grieved so terribly that his black hair turned snow white and he shrank two inches in height.

Why across the river, I wonder? I look down and see a narrow cement road, the width of a bullock cart and at water level, crosses to the opposite bank. My nerve ending on the map is this simple stretch of cement. Life below is as ageless as on the other rivers. On the steps far below the palace, women wash their clothes, buffaloes wallow like shining black islands and boys dive and swim. To the north, as the river curves away, are two small white temples; and when I lift my eyes, through the shadows I can see the outline of Asirgarh.

Why across the river? To look upon her as he dwelt in the palace. Isn't that why he built the Taj Mahal too, across a different river so he could look upon her? This palace and that tomb could not reflect the splendour and magnificence of Shah Jahan. There's no stone here to sculpt, nothing except brick and so he left it as it is. Six months after she died and was buried here, he sent his son Murad to disinter her and carry her body back up to Agra where she was buried in a temporary tomb until the Taj Mahal was ready for her. Briefly, in death as in life, she led a nomadic existence, but then as the marble sarcophagus settled down with her, eternity claimed her forever.

The connection between where I stand and the remainder of the palace has broken and we have to return to the road and circle round. In the shadow of trees stretches a low, long building which too looks palace-like, except the board proclaims this is the Archaeological Department. A peon springs up from his stool outside the office and approaches, proclaiming he is a guide.

'Come with me, Sahib,' he says, 'I'll show you the hamam of the empress Mumtaz Mahal. It is where she did her toilet.'

He leads us to the last room in the building and with a great flourish pulls out keys and unlocks the door. I suspect it shouldn't be locked in the first place.

'You must not tell the director I'm showing you this place,' he whispers and we step into a dark and gloomy chamber.

As our sight gradually adjusts to the gloom, the walls spring to life with beautiful designs in bright colours and in the floor is a sunken tub. The peon takes out a match box and strikes a light and the room comes ablaze. Inset into the designs, along the walls and the ceiling, are thousands of small mirrors. The yellow flame is caught and reflected from every corner, and then darkness comes again.

'She could look upon herself as she was bathed,' he whispers with a salacious grin. 'And come, I'll show you where she was first buried.'

'We know,' I say and he waits ingratiatingly for a tip before shutting the door behind us once more.

The broken wing of the palace juts further out towards the river but no nearer the grave.

'Why don't you go over to it?' Maureen asks. 'We'll wait here.'

Wisely, she knows this is my own private pilgrimage. I, like a little god, will recreate her life for my own use in my novel; and recreate her death. It would not be difficult to reach that grave. From where I stand, I can see the narrow pathway zig-zagging down to the river's bank, and then along the bank to the strip of cement, caressed by water. It would take five minutes to cross and then a walk up the dusty road. A wheat field would separate me from the grave but I could see how I would skirt, and then I would stand in the shadow of her first tomb.

'Not now, not just yet.' Darkness is swiftly descending and already her grave is creeping back into shadows, fading from view.

'Well, where are we going to spend the night then?' Nalini asks pragmatically.

'There's a dak bungalow somewhere here, and there must be a hotel.'

'Hotel!' Nalini sniffs in disbelief. 'Where do you think you are? Delhi? This is Burhanpur.'

I am eternally optimistic about such things. However, I cannot leave this place just yet, it has taken a hold of me, even its desolation has its own beauty. We return to stand in the empty and nameless chamber, watching the sun setting. The sky is streaked with great sketches of red and gold and the sun is a contemplatable red ball slowly falling below the horizon. The grave has retreated into shadow and is no longer visible. I only imagine it still stands there as it has done for centuries in front of that same grove of trees.

It is time to retreat and we find our driver and ask him to take us to the dak bungalow. He claims to know where it is but, no longer trusting his knowledge, I get directions. It is about a mile outside the town walls, hidden behind a barbed wire fence and set in a pleasant, well tended garden. As we turn into the drive, a policeman lounging by the steps, snaps to attention and barks out a command. A dozen other cops, lugging .303 rifles, struggle out from the bushes, line up and snap to attention. The sergeant snaps the car a rigid salute and holds the pose until I get out of the car. His spine crumbles, his hand flaps down like a broken wing, the men melt back into the shadows. The exhilaration is over too quick for me to appreciate the moment. A portly bearer saunters out and stands looking down on me from the steps.

'What was that about?'

'There are two ministers visiting here. They thought you were them.'

'Is there room here?'

He looks patient. 'No, Sir. There are two ministers visiting here.'

Nalini sticks her head out of the window. 'See, I told you.' She asks the bearer, 'Is there a decent hotel where we can stay?'

'In town there is.' He can't remember the name but he gives the driver instructions to find it.

'Maybe we should phone,' Nalini suggests and the bearer

ambles in and brings out the very slim telephone directory. He remembers the hotel name and disappears to call them, but only to return a moment later.

'Telephone out of order,' he intones.

We return to old Burhanpur, the driver following his explicit directions, and come to a stop at a very crowded street corner. All we can see is a chemist's shop. I crane my neck around. 'Where's the hotel?' Nalini asks.

'There, above the chemist.'

We can see a narrow balcony and a couple of rooms behind. An old board proclaims those rooms are a hotel.

'They look okay,' I murmur tentatively, knowing we can't return to Indore now. The driver refuses to make the journey at night as he wisely values his life too dearly. 'Besides, I want to stay.'

'They don't,' Nalini says abruptly. 'I'm not going to stay in that place. God knows what I'll catch.'

Maureen remains wisely quiet while brother and sister bicker. It appears this is the only hotel in town and there is no other. We lapse into frustrated silence.

'Well,' I say, breaking it, 'I do have the name of someone here called Brigadier Gerewal.'

Nalini stares at me in total astonishment. 'You mean to say, brother dear, we have been sitting here in this stupid car staring at this stupid hotel for ten minutes and you now say you know someone in Burhanpur?'

'I don't know him. A general I met in Delhi gave me his name.'

'Well, that's enough, for God's sake.' She is proud of her restraint at this moment as darkness certainly has descended on Burhanpur. I suspect if we were children, I would have received a whack on the head. 'Go and call him.'

The chemist has a telephone and we look up my Brigadier's telephone number. I have an address: The Tapti Mills, and not much more. The chemist finds the number and dials. We get no reply, even after a dozen tries.

'How far is the mill?' I ask.

'Up that road, Sir.'

That is direction enough for Nalini. She commands the driver to take off up the road and a mile further up, we come upon a huge mill. It lies behind a neatly cultivated garden, a barbed wire fence and a couple of very military-looking security men.

'Is Brigadier Gerewal here?'

'Who is asking for him?'

I start to ramble into a detailed explanation when Nalini intervenes, understanding India far better than I.

'Give him your card.'

I find a bent and cracked one, and hand it to the security man who calls up someone or the other on his telephone and then comes out of his sentry box. The barrier lifts and we are directed towards a very pleasant-looking bungalow.

A tall, immaculately-dressed, ramrod-straight Sikh gentleman awaits us at the entrance. I introduce ourselves, my sister now playing subdued Indian woman, and the Brigadier immediately ushers us into the veranda. India is a place where we recognize each other immediately, even if we have never met and come from distant parts of the planetary system. We are the sort of people he would have known in Delhi or Meerut or Simla or wherever he has been posted during his army days. He speaks English with that clipped Sandhurst military accent. He mulls over our problem.

'You could stay with me but unfortunately my wife is away and it will be difficult for me to look after you. I'm "batching it" at the moment.' He strokes his fine beard. 'You can stay in the guest house if you don't object.'

'That'll be fine,' Nalini pounces. 'And thank you very much, Sir.'

Bearers materialize and we are led up to the larger of the two bungalows. The rooms are clean and spacious and comfortably furnished. The Brigadier hovers behind us.

'You see there is only one bedroom spare. This is actually the director's suite. You can all either sleep in the bedroom or I'll have the bearers put beds out in the veranda.'

'Is it safe?'

'Oh, of course. We have 24-hour security.'

'Then we can sleep out.'

Beds too materialize, as does hot water in the bathrooms, spouting and belching from old geysers, and a dinner ordered for us.

'Why are you here? We don't often see travellers in Burhanpur.'

'We came to see Arjumand's first grave.'

He raises an eyebrow. 'Not many people know about it.' He sighs. 'And that old palace has been totally neglected by the Archaeological Department. It is of great historical interest to us all. But apart from that grave and palace, Burhanpur is also important for us Sikhs. One of our gurus' tombs is here too, just outside Burhanpur. The government should bring tourists down here instead of just Agra, Delhi, Jaipur. There is so much to see.'

We have also one other thing in common with this courteous Sikh gentleman. Our father. An army man will recognize these two army brats and my sister's memory, the stronger, stirs and spins out our travels as children in the van of the Indian army. The older one, she was naturally more aware of her surroundings then, while for me they emerge but dimly: clambering into the back of army trucks, gorging myself on English sweets and chewing gum, the rough hewn army uniform of my father and the weight of his army revolver in my childhood hands. The friends we knew in those pre-Independence days were later, post-Independence, to become chiefs of army staff, Generals and Field Marshals. But my father, commissioned by King George VI, quit before Independence and returned to civilian life. He was never truly cut out to be a soldier.

The Brigadier was in communications and posted not merely around India but the troubled spots of the world as an advisor. But most of his days were spent on the border of our truncated wing, Pakistan.

How many armies have marched and counter-marched across India over these past centuries. Countless. Greek, Persian, Turk, Mongol, Mughal, English, French, Portuguese, Maharajah this, Nawab that and it is this great out-pouring of warriors, like the many streams down an ancient mountain that have been fashioned into this modern one—the Indian army. The past is to be found scattered around within this single force—a Greek here, a Mughal there, an Anglo-Indian, a Jat, a Dogra, a Sikh, a Tamil. The British hammered and honed the diversity of a people and of a history into one identity, an awesome achievement that survived their own passing. The army exists in another country to India; it lives a separate life, private and ordered. You can actually see this different country as you travel India—an oasis of neat fences and walls, gardens and barracks, spit and polish, ceremony and splendour. There is bloodshed too, behind those walls and ceremonies. Three wars with Pakistan won; one with China, lost. It is a private world, in whichever country, that describes all us outsiders as 'civilians'. The Indian army is as British as the British left it in 1947. The weaponry might have changed, MIGs instead of Spitfires, missiles instead of cannons, but their social customs have remained unchanged. There must be in India even a special school for the army which coaches them to speak in Sandhurst accents.

'I was coming up to retirement,' he tells us in the dim glow of electric bulbs, 'and I was offered this job as managing director of the mill. Naturally I knew nothing about mills but I was used to commanding men.' He sighs heavily. 'It is so difficult dealing with civilians. In the army when I gave an order, it was immediately executed. Here I keep a note of my orders and the number of times I have to remind my subordinates to carry them out.'

I can quite understand the Brigadier's frustrations at dealing with civilians, especially in the Indian industrial world. He has moved from the steely interior discipline of military men into the noisy, chaotic one of politics and power. The unions that control the industrial workers are for the most part run by lawyer-politicians and if it is to their advantage to strike, to gherao, and use other various weaponry of civilian strife peculiar to India, they do. Industry is comparatively new to Indian life. Our British rulers deliberately stunted our industrial aspirations in order to protect their own factories and workers in England. We were kept rural and forced to purchase everything from a sewing needle to a motor car from the English factories. And when we first tried to industrialize under their patronizing stares, we were told we were incapable of running factories or understanding technology. It is only since our Independence that the boom in industrialization has taken place and we race pell-mell to catch up with a revolution that is already nearly passed in the Western countries. For the first time in centuries, we are not confined to the fields and have the lucrative alternative of factory work, making those same sewing needles and motor cars, locomotives and fighter jets, computers and televisions. And for millions of factory workers and their union leaders, this is a Klondike of opportunity and manipulation.

'Do you have many problems?' I ask the Brigadier.

'When I first came I did. Every second day there'd be a strike because this wasn't right or that. So I decided I had to have a strategy. I spent my days moving through the factory and when a man complained to me about the latrines not being cleaned or this not being done, I'd make a note and get that done if their complaint was legitimate. They got to know I was a man of action and of my word. I also pinpointed the union troublemakers. Three men. It all came to a head one day when they decided to gherao me here over some problem. They surrounded me and began to shout their slogans. Each time they stopped, I insisted they continue shouting and I wouldn't let any one of them leave the gherao. I was determined to outlast them, and I did. I showed them I wasn't afraid nor was I going to be intimidated by their childish tactics. After that, I fired the three troublemakers and since then we've had relative peace in the mill.'

Nalini is struck into awed silence. Her doctor husband works for a tyre factory in Madras and her experiences of industrial strife are very personal. Strikes, drunkenness, bullying of management, gheraoes, whatever.

'That's all it takes,' she finally announces, having found the Holy Grail. 'Guts. None of the stupid people who run our factories have any guts.'

The Brigadier is modest. 'People want to be treated fairly but they mustn't be allowed to take advantage in their numbers.' He stands up to take his leave. 'You must make a tour of the mill tomorrow. Now I have some work to get done but what time will you breakfast with me?'

I cannot sleep easily. I stand on the balcony looking out on Burhanpur, unbelieving that I've finally come to this ancient town. What lies around me here is the modern India, nestled against that old walled town a few miles back up the road. Arjumand passed close by, Shah Jahan stood in that spot below me, Akbar there, Aurangzeb here. We cannot truly see a place until we know the past intimately; otherwise ruins and forts become mere sights, one-dimensional objects that do not vibrate through our consciousness. At the break of dawn, I wake the driver and drive back to the palace.

At this cool, light time of the day the old town is just beginning to stir and the palace stands chilly and deserted, sightlessly watching the roll of the Tapti. The grave begins another day of solitude on earth, protecting nothing, marking nothing but memory. I sit on a parapet, staring across, looking down too at the descending path and the concrete strip across the river. I imagine myself walking down, wetting my bare feet in the Tapti, then along that dusty road and across the bund to stand by the monument and feel its shadow fall over me. I came all this way to do just that and I can't move. I remain rooted to this parapet, not wanting to ever complete the journey, as if knowing the ending always brings disillusionment. Like the end of a love affair, the dregs of sadness.

A portly man, a Bania figure, disturbs my solitude. He ignores me to start walking. Up and down the palace floor, a daily exercise, treading on top of the footsteps of kings and queens. He unsettles me with his indifference, his single-minded purpose, oblivious to his surroundings. The sun comes up, burning my face, heating the stones so they come to life and hurt. I cannot sit here, not with this man pacing.

The path down is steep, almost vertical, past the honeycomb of broken rooms, past garbage and goat shit and human shit. I reach the river bank and pass women starting their morning chores of washing cooking utensils and clothes and sleepy children defecating. A bullock cart rumbles down to the concrete strip ahead of me and the driver turns to watch me follow. The cool water, gently flowing over, cleanses my feet of dust. To the far left, just as the river curves, are a couple of small white temples, peaceful and tranquil; while to the right a couple of buffaloes roll in the water. The road on the far side climbs abruptly, dusty, cracked, and ridged from bullock carts. I decide to walk along the river bank, skirting the wheat field. The ruined palace looks like a skeleton, hollow and broken. I glimpse the white dressed figure of my Bania, still pacing, working off his cholesterol. The tomb increases in height, appears to swell as I approach. The illusion of the Taj Mahal is that from the main gateway, you think it isn't large; as you approach, it turns gigantic. This one has no such illusion except the one of distance. I stand in its shadow finally. It looks so undistinguished, the tomb of a minor Muslim landlord. The brick face is black with age and when I touch, it feels hoary. My fingers are darkened. I circle it. It is one-dimensional; a wall set down in a field. Once, hundreds of years ago, it stood in a garden. Why, I wonder, wasn't it demolished?

An old man, tending the wheat field, has been watching me and now, unable to curb his curiosity, slowly, deferentially approaches to stand a few feet away. The skin of his hands is cracked and worn, and the weather and hardship have cut deep seams in his face; darkened it too. I cannot tell his age, he seems ageless.

'Do you know what this is?' I ask him.

He studies me and then the tomb, as if noticing it for the first time and appraising its presence. He folds his arms and returns to looking at me. He says,

'It is the first tomb of the Great Rani. When she died, her husband, the king Shah Jahan, buried her here. He was very grieved by her death and there, in the palace, he wept for many days. I heard no one could move, no one could breathe during his mourning and we could not work in the fields or buy food even. And then, many months later, he sent his youngest son with men to dig her body up and carry her coffin north to bury her in the proper tomb he began building for her there, the Mumtaj Mahal. I have not yet seen it but I have heard it is beautiful. It is made of marble and gold and silver and diamonds…the true tears of a king.'

Epilogue

Swiftly, we are back in Indore and at the gates of the Hotel Suhag. They are locked and four policemen sit on the ground beyond, playing cards. The driver honks and they ignore us and when I get out to unlock the gate, I find it has been sealed.

'What's happened?'

'The government has taken the building,' a policeman finally replies. 'You cannot enter.'

'But our luggage? My helmet…'

'My table,' Nalini wails.

They return to their card game, and it is only a passer-by who tells us that the government official even now, on this Sunday, is sitting in a bungalow behind the silent hotel. We follow his directions along the wall and find it. He turns out to be a small, bespectacled man, wearing white; polite but unhelpful.

'Wait,' is all he says when we demand our luggage.

'But what happened?'

'They did not pay their taxes so we seized the hotel.'

'How much?' Nalini demands.

'Twenty-one lakhs,' the official replies.

'Twenty-one lakhs! My God, if I don't pay my few

thousand you people are down on my neck threatening to drag me off to jail. And these people you allow to run up a bill of twenty-one lakhs.'

The official looks unconcerned, his fingertips join, making a temple. We wait, and wait. Other officials, one a magistrate from Bhopal, bustle in and out. They eat lunch, smoke cigarettes, chatter between each other, and our increasing bad tempers only elicit smiles and further 'waits'.

Finally, we are summoned. I am handed a blank sheet of paper and ordered to take down his dictation. 'Your full name and address.' I write that down. Then, 'I have received my luggage and find it all intact with nothing missing…'

'But I haven't received my luggage.'

'Soon. It is all upstairs.'

I fume and write, absolving him, the government, of all responsibility. Nalini too has to write the same letter. When we have signed and been duly witnessed, we're led up the stairs to a room in which our luggage has been flung in a corner. My helmet is intact and Nalini's table. Maureen is missing a couple of small items—'phoren' makeup and shampoo.

Four hours have passed since we arrived and the luggage has been here all along. All three of us scream at the officials. They look mournfully puzzled at our frustration.

'I will complain about you.'

'Why? We are only doing our duty and you have your luggage.'

All journeys end in such anti-climaxes. I had my research notes, the geography of that distant past and all I had to do was write the novel. Arjumand had to be the central character; I had to bring her to life from the marble tomb. That took months until one day I found her voice…

Arjumand:

Was it thunder that woke me? I sat up, listening. It was not yet the monsoon season, but the air was tense with that same sense of expectancy, and still, as if waiting to rage. I could hear nothing, except the first caw of crows, the bul-bul practising its enchanting scales, and squirrels scolding shrilly. The sky was pale and clear with the smoke of night still lingering on the edges of the horizon. The mango and peepul and banyan trees outside the window appeared transparent in the delicate light.

It might have been my dream that woke me…

ALSO BY SPEAKING TIGER

GULBADAN: PORTRAIT OF A PRINCESS AT A MUGHAL COURT

Rumer Godden

An accomplished scholar and author of the *Humayun-nama*, Gulbadan Begam was also Babur's daughter, Humayun's sister, and Akbar's aunt.

In this compact biography, Rumer Godden draws upon the *Humayun-nama* and other records, as well as her own soaring imagination, to create a portrait of the begam and the Mughal Empire as detailed and exquisite as any miniature.

While still a child, Gulbadan travelled from Kabul to Agra, where Babur had established his capital. She grew up in the cloistered world of the zenana, an idyllic existence that was shattered when Babur exchanged his life for Humayun's. Humayun's reign was marked by hardship after he lost the Empire and his vast army was reduced to a ragtag band. The Empire was regained but, soon after, Humayun died in a freak accident. He was succeeded by Akbar and it was under him that the Mughal Empire reached its zenith, in territory and in cultural and religious accomplishments.

This rich, broad sweep of history, written from Gulbadan's point of view, is interspersed with colourful re-creations of goings-on within the zenana and the many diversions and internecine politics of the royal court.

Combining a historian's rigour with a novelist's gift for invention, *Gulbadan* is a timeless classic.

ALSO BY SPEAKING TIGER

BELLS OF SHANGRI-LA: SCHOLARS, SPIES, INVADERS IN TIBET

Parimal Bhattacharya

Almost all of the Himalaya had been mapped by the time the Great Game—in which the British and Russian Empires fought for control of Central and Southern Asia—reached its zenith in the latter half of the 19th century. Only Tibet remained unknown and unexplored, zealously guarded and closed off to everyone. Britain sent a number of spies into this forbidden land, disguised as pilgrims and wanderers, outfitted with secret survey equipment and not much else. These intrepid explorers were tasked with collecting topographical knowledge, and information about the culture and customs of Tibet.

Among the many who were sent was Kinthup, a tailor who went as a monk's companion to confirm that the Tsangpo and the Brahmaputra were the same river. In an arduous mission that lasted four years, Kinthup had many adventures—he was even sold as a slave by the monk—before he returned, having succeeded, only to find that the officers who had sent him, and the family he left behind, were all dead.

Sarat Chandra Das, a schoolmaster, also went on a clandestine mission. He came back in two years, having compiled extensive data and carrying a trove of ancient manuscripts and documents. He went on to become a renowned Tibetologist and Buddhist scholar.

Bells of Shangri-La brings to vivid life the journeys and adventures of Kinthup, Sarat Chandra Das and others, including Eric Bailey, an officer who was part of the British invasion of Tibet in 1903, and who later followed in Kinthup's footsteps to the Tsangpo. Weaving biography with precise historical knowledge, and the memories of his own treks over some of the trails covered by these travellers, Parimal Bhattacharya writes in the great tradition of Peter Hopkirk and Peter Matthiessen to create a sparkling, unprecedented work of non-fiction.